Workbook

French

Débutants

Estelle Demontrond-Box

About this workbook

Designed for beginners in French, the 20 lessons in this workbook, which contain some 200 exercises, will allow you to progressively learn and practice the fundamentals of the language, from pronunciation and vocabulary through to simple sentence construction.

Each lesson deals with a key grammatical point such as verb conjugation and usage, parts of speech or sentence structure, as well as giving pronunciation tips. The exercises allow active and contextual reinforcement of the points covered, calling upon what you've learned about the language. The aim of the workbook is to provide a fun and systematic way to learn French.

As you work through the exercises, you can self-assess your results by selecting the appropriate icon after each exercise (☺ if the majority of your answers were correct, 😐 if around half of your answers were correct, or ☹ if less than half were correct). After a lesson, enter the number of icons of each type you received in the exercises, and then enter these totals into the final score table at the end of the workbook so you can tally your final results after completing all the exercises.

Note: the phonetic transcription used in this workbook was created by the author and simplified for beginners. The transcriptions may therefore differ slightly from those used in other ASSIMIL publications.

Contents

Alphabet & pronunciation

(accents, silent letters, liaison)

The alphabet *(L'alphabet)*

The French alphabet is the same as the English alphabet, although some of the names of the letters are pronounced differently (see below).

A [ah]	**G** [jzay]	**M** [em]	**S** [es]	**Y** [eegrek]
B [bay]	**H** [ash]	**N** [en]	**T** [tay]	**Z** [zed]
C [say]	**I** [ee]	**O** [oh]	**U** [ew]	
D [day]	**J** [jzee]	**P** [pay]	**V** [vay]	
E [uh]	**K** [kah]	**Q** [kew]	**W** [doobluh vay]	
F [ef]	**L** [el]	**R** [er]	**X** [eeks]	

- Note that the French letters **g** and **j** are swapped compared to the English pronunciation. (Also, the initial [zh] sound is similar to the 's' in *measure.*) Another difference is the letter **w**, which in French is a 'double v' as opposed to a 'double u'.
- To pronounce the French letter **u** [ew], purse your lips while saying [ee]. The result should sound something like the 'u' in *refuse*.

Greetings *(Les salutations)*

bonjour [boh^{n}jzoor]	*good morning / good afternoon*
salut [salew]	*hello / hi*
bonsoir [boh^{n}swar]	*good evening*
bonne nuit [bon new-ee]	*good night*
à bientôt [a bya^{n}toh]	*see you soon* (**bientôt** *soon*)
au revoir [oh ruhvwar]	*goodbye*
monsieur [muhsee-uh]	*Mr, sir*
madame [madam]	*Mrs, madam*
mademoiselle [madmwazehl]	*miss*
Je m'appelle... [jzuh mapehl]	*My name is ...*
bienvenue [bya^{n}vuhnew]	*welcome*
Ça va ? [sa va]	*How are things?*

In the wordbanks, the **red** letters are silent.

1 **Spell these French first names aloud with the help of the letters on the previous page.**

M-A-R-T-I-N-E
X-A-V-I-E-R

G-I-L-L-E-S

J-O-S-E-P-H
P-A-T-R-I-C-K

Note that if a vowel takes an accent, this is also the case for capital letters: *Élise.*

Saint's names

France is traditionally a Catholic country, and each day of the year has an associated saint's name. Those who are named after a saint are sometimes offered a small gift or card on their saint's day.

2 **Match each French word or phrase to its English equivalent.**

MONSIEUR | AU REVOIR | BONJOUR | BONNE NUIT | MADEMOISELLE | SALUT | À BIENTÔT

GOOD MORNING | HI | GOOD NIGHT | SEE YOU SOON | SIR | GOODBYE | MISS

3 **Put the letters in the right order in each of these words you've learned. Then write the meaning in English.**

E.g. leeelmmadsio → **mademoiselle** = miss

a. lstau → .... =..

b. sioobrn → .... =..

c. aeammd → .... =..

d. ttnbieô → .... =..

e. eeevnnibu → .... =..

French written accents *(Les accents français)*

Certain letters in French have accents, which usually indicate how it is pronounced:

- The acute accent (**l'accent aigu**) **é** is used on the vowel **e** to show it is pronounced [ay].
- The grave accent (**l'accent grave**) **è** is mainly used on the vowel **e** to show it is pronounced [eh]. It can also be used on **a** or **u** to distinguish words that otherwise look alike, without changing the pronunciation (e.g. **à** *to, at* and **a** [*he/she/it*] *has*).
- The circumflex accent (**l'accent circonflexe**) **^** can be used on the vowels **a**, **e**, **i**, **o** and **u**. It changes the pronunciation slightly on certain letters, but beginners don't need to worry about this!
- The ¨ (**le tréma**) is used to indicate that a vowel must be pronounced separately rather than blended with another vowel: **Noël** [noh-el].
- Finally, the cedilla (**la cédille**) is a little hook at the bottom of the letter **c**, which indicates it is pronounced [s] as in **ça** *this, that*.

Some French holidays *(Quelques fêtes françaises)*

Pâques [pak]	*Easter*
Noël [noehl]	*Christmas*
la Pentecôte [la pah^{n}tkoht]	*Pentecost*
la Fête nationale [la feht nasyonal]	*Bastille Day* (14th of July)
la fête des Mères/Pères [la feht day mehr/pehr]	*Mother's / Father's Day* (**la mère** *mother*, **le père** *father*, **la fête** *celebration)*
l'Épiphanie [laypeefanee]	*Epiphany*
la fête du Travail [la feht dew trava-ee]	*Labour Day*
la Toussaint [la toosa^{n}]	*All Saints' Day*

Time off

The French have 11 official public holidays, including 6 based on Catholic festivals.

4 Spell these French celebrations aloud, including the accents.

a. P-Â-Q-U-E-S
b. N-O-Ë-L
c. P-E-N-T-E-C-Ô-T-E
d. É-P-I-P-H-A-N-I-E
e. P-È-R-E-S

5 **Circle the right spelling for each word in the sentences below, then write their meaning (using a dictionary if you need to).**

a. àge / age / âge ....

b. être / étre / ètre..

c. frere / frère / frére ....

d. salüt / salut / salût ....

e. Fransse / Françe / France ....

f. français / francais / franscais..............................

g. féte / fête / fète ....

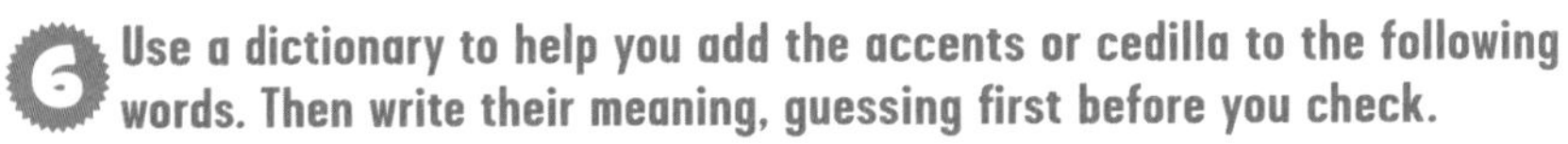

6 **Use a dictionary to help you add the accents or cedilla to the following words. Then write their meaning, guessing first before you check.**

a. pere = ...

b. aout = ...

c. lecon = ...

d. Suede = ...

e. canoe = ...

f. americain = ...

Silent letters in French *(Les lettres muettes en français)*

Unfortunately, French is rarely pronounced as it is written. Certain letters are not even pronounced at all! This often occurs at the end of words, such as with final consonants (**salut** *hi* [sahlew]) and the silent **e** (**femme** *woman* [fam]). It also occurs with the letter **h**, which is always silent (**homme** *man* [ohm]).

Numbers from 0 to 10 ***(Les nombres de 0 à 10)***

0 to 10			
zéro [zayroh]	*zero*	**six** [sees]	*six*
un [a^n]	*one*	**sept** [seht]	*seven*
deux [duh]	*two*	**huit** [ew-eet]	*eight*
trois [trwa]	*three*	**neuf** [nuhf]	*nine*
quatre [katr]	*four*	**dix** [dees]	*ten*
cinq [sa^{n}k]	*five*		

7 **Read these French words and their meanings. Then read them aloud (the red letters are silent).**

estomac *stomach*	**salut** *hi*	**abricot** *apricot*	**nerf** *nerve*	**trop** *too much*
deux *two*	**outil** *tool*	**trois** *three*	**mot** *word*	**froid** *cold*

8 **Match each French word to the corresponding number.**

deux zéro dix neuf cinq huit sept

9 5 8 7 2 10 0

Liaison *(La liaison)*

- A liaison in French is when a consonant that is normally silent at the end of one word is pronounced at the beginning of the following word. Liaisons usually occur between two words when the first ends with a consonant and the second starts with a vowel: **un enfant** *a child* [a^n nah^{n}fah^n].
- The letters **s**, **x**, **z**, **t**, **d**, **n** and **m**, which are normally silent at the end of a word, are sometimes pronounced if the following word starts with a vowel sound or a mute **h**: **les hommes** *the men* [leh zohm].
- Note that an **s** is pronounced [z] in a liaison.

9 **Read the following phrases aloud, making the liaison as indicated in the phonetic pronunciations in brackets.**

deux amis [duh zahmee]
(**ami** *friend*)

trois oncles [trwah zoh^{n}kl]
(**oncle** *uncle*)

six hôtels [see zohtehl]

un éléphant [a^n naylayfah^n]

un petit enfant [a^n puhtee tah^{n}fah^n]
(**petit** *small*)

un grand homme [a^n grah^n tom]
(**grand** *tall* or *important*)

 **Complete the crossword using the French words you've learned so far.** 

	1	2	3	4	5	6	7	8	9	10	11	12	13
A													
B													
C													
D													
E													
F													
G									N			E	U
H									E				
I													
J													
K													
L													

Here are the clues in English:

Horizontal

A. three
B. age
D. good morning
F. zero
G. American (masc.) – had (past participle)
H. nine
I. one
J. Christmas
L. ten

Vertical

1. friend (masc.)
3. two
5. Mr, sir
8. five
9. hi – not (… *pas*)
11. cold
12. mother
13. tool

Well done! You've reached the end of Lesson 1. It's time to count up how many of each type of icon you received. Then record your results here and in the final assessment table on page 127.

2 More on pronunciation

(nasal vowels and semi-consonants, the French r and u)

Key sounds in French

French sound	English equivalent
sa, là, femme, pâte	[a], an [a] in between pat and father
thé, ses	[ay] as in say
baguette, chaise, ouvert	[eh] as in bet
île, si	[ee] as in beet
homme, drôle, bateau	[o] as in open
où, pour	[oo] as in food
me, sœur, jeune, peu	[uh] as in about
tu	[ew] as in refuse (to make this sound, purse the lips while pronouncing [ee])
ouest, oui	[w] as in wet or week
yeux, billet	[y] as in yes
travail	[a]-[ee] as in fight
abeille	[eh]-[ee] as in laying
policier	[ee]-[ay], but said quickly sounds like [yay]
bière	[ee]-[eh], but said quickly sounds like [yeh]
vieux	[ee]-[uh], but said quickly sounds like [yuh]
grenouille	[oo]-[ee] as in gooey
feuille	[uh]-[ee]
nuit	[ew]-[ee], as in few + week, and said quickly sounds similar to [wee]

French sound	English equivalent
balle	[b] as in ball
carte, kaki, quart	[k] as in cat (the u after q is often silent)
chou, shampooing	[sh] as in shin or bush
danse	[d] as in dot
frère, photo	[f] as in father
garage	[g] as in goat
jour	[jz] as in vision
homme	h before a vowel is silent
lampe	[l] as in lamp
mère	[m] as in mother
nez	[n] as in near
ligne	[ny] as in canyon
père	[p] as in pot
rouge	[r] guttural r as in the Scottish word loch
sous, place, ça, option, dix	[s] as in sit
tortue	[t] as in turtle
vert	[v] as in verb
zéro, dix-huit, vase	[z] as in zoo
blanc, champ, embrasse, son, vin, loin	vowels or diphthongs* followed by n or m are nasalized: pronounce the vowel as if it was followed by [ng] (for example, song): [ah^n], [oh^n], [a^n], [wa^n] etc.

* A diphthong is a combination of vowels that are pronounced as a single syllable, in which the sound begins as one vowel and blends into the next.

Numbers from 11 to 22
(Les nombres de 11 à 22)

11 to 22	
onze [oh^{n}z]	*eleven*
douze [dooz]	*twelve*
treize [trehz]	*thirteen*
quatorze [katorz]	*fourteen*
quinze [ka^{n}z]	*fifteen*
seize [sehz]	*sixteen*
dix-sept [deeseht]	*seventeen*
dix-huit [deezew-eet]	*eighteen*
dix-neuf [deeznuhf]	*nineteen*
vingt [va^n]	*twenty*
vingt et un [va^{n}teh-a^n]	*twenty-one*
vingt-deux [va^{n}tduh]	*twenty-two*

Note: the numbers from 23 to 29 follow the same pattern as 22.

1 **Use the phonetic transcription to write the French word (use the table on the previous page if you need to) and then write the English equivalent.**

a. [salew] = ... = ...

b. [amee] = ... = ...

c. [mehr] = ... = ...

d. [katr] = ... = ...

e. [moh] = ... = ...

f. [amayreeka^n] = ...

= ....

2 **Unscramble the letters to write these numbers in French and then write the English equivalents.**

a. éorz = ... = ...

b. rqazoute = ... = ...

c. iuth = ... = ...

d. xdi-fune = ... = ...

e. tnigv = ... = ...

f. eerzit = ... = ...

Nasal vowels and semi-consonants *(Voyelles nasales et semi-consonnes)*

In French syllables ending in **m** or **n**, the vowel sound is nasalized. The **m** or **n** is silent, and the preceding vowel sound is pronounced in a way similar to a vowel followed by *ng* in English, as in *song* (**train** [tra^n] *train*, **oncle** [oh^{n}kl] *uncle*). Here are some examples of nasal vowel sounds in French:

- **en/em**: [ah^n] (**trente** [trah^{n}t] *thirty*)
- **an/am**: [ah^n] (**tante** [tah^{n}t] *aunt*)
- **ain/aim/ein/eim/in/im/un/um**: [a^n] (**vingt** [va^n] *twenty*, **pain** [pa^n] *bread*, **plein** [pla^n] *full*, **brun** [bra^n] *brown*, **rien** [ree-a^n] *nothing*)
- **on/om**: [oh^n] (**garçon** [garsoh^n] *boy*, **tomber** [toh^{n}bay] *to fall*)

Semi-consonants (or semi-vowels)

In some contexts, certain diphthongs are pronounced like consonants:

- **ui**: [ew-ee] (**huit** [ew-eet] *eight*)
- **ail**: [a-yee] (**travail** [trava-ee-ay] *work*)
- **ou**: [w] (**oui** [wee] *yes*)

Family *(La famille)*

la mère [mehr]	*mother*	**le mari** [maree]	*husband*
le père [pehr]	*father*	**le cousin** [kooza^n]	*cousin* (m.)
le frère [frehr]	*brother*	**la cousine** [koozeen]	*cousin* (f.)
la sœur [suhr]	*sister*	**l'oncle** [oh^{n}kl]	*uncle*
le fils [fees]	*son*	**la tante** [tah^{n}t]	*aunt*
la fille [fee-y]	*daughter*	**le grand-père** [grah^n pehr]	*grandfather*
la femme [fam]	*wife*	**la grand-mère** [grah^n mehr]	*grandmother*

3 **Underline the nasal vowel sound in each word and then write its phonetic pronunciation as shown in the example.**

E.g. cinq = cinq = [a^n]

a. onze ....
b. à demain *(see you tomorrow)*.................
c. tante ....
d. faim *(hunger)* ....
e. chacun *(each)* ....
f. bonjour ....
g. patin *(skate)* ....
h. parfum ....

4 **Use the phonetic transcription to write the French word and then write the English equivalent.**

a. [suhr] = ... = ...
b. [dooz] = ... = ...
c. [grah^n pehr] = ... = ...
d. [ah^{n}fah^n] = ... = ...
e. [sa^{n}k] = ... = ...
f. [oh^{n}kl] = ... = ...

The [u] sound *(Le son [u])*

As the French **u** sound doesn't exist in English, it is often mispronounced as [oo]. To practice the correct pronunciation, purse your lips while saying [ee]. The result is a bit like [ew] as in *few*.

5 **Practice your pronunciation of the French *u* [ew] by saying the following words aloud.**

a. tu (*you*) **b.** salut **c.** musique **d.** bus **e.** flûte

6 Practice the pronunciation of the French *u* [ew] and *ou* [oo] sounds.

a. **tutu**
b. **toute** (*all* [sing. fem.])
c. **jour** (*day*)
d. **futur**
e. **douze**

The [r] sound *(Le son [r])*

The French **r** is another sound that doesn't exist in English and is particularly tricky for learners of the language. It is a guttural sound similar to the Spanish **j** or the Scottish **ch** as in *Loch Ness*. To pronounce it, place the base of your tongue at the back of your throat and the tip of your tongue behind the lower teeth as you say **r**. This takes some practice, but you'll get there!

7 Practice the pronunciation of the French *r* by saying these words aloud. 

a. bonjour **b.** trois **c.** au revoir **d.** quatre **e.** être

8 Look at the picture and then write the name of each family member. 

La mère : ....

La sœur : ....

Le père : ....

La grand-mère : ....

Le frère : ....

Le grand-père : ....

Excellent! You've reached the end of Lesson 2. Count up the icons from the exercises and record your result here and in the final evaluation table on page 127.

3

Nouns & articles

(masculine/feminine, singular/plural)

Masculine and feminine nouns *(Les noms masculins et féminins)*

- In French, all nouns have a gender – masculine (m.) or feminine (f.) – even if they refer to things and not people. In the latter case, a noun ending in a consonant that refers to a male (e.g. **cousin**) is often turned into a feminine noun to refer to a female by adding **-e** (e.g. **cousin<u>e</u>**). However, there are exceptions.
- For other nouns, when you learn a new word, try to remember its gender!

House and rooms *(La maison et les pièces)*

la chambre (f.) [la shah^{n}br]	*bedroom*
la cuisine (f.) [la kew-eezeen]	*kitchen*
le garage (m.) [luh garajz]	*garage*
le grenier (m.) [luh gruhnee-ay]	*attic*
le jardin (m.) [luh jzarda^n]	*garden*
la salle à manger (f.) [la sal a mah^{n}jzay]	*dining room*
la salle de bain (f.) [la sal duh ba^n]	*bathroom*
le salon (m.) [luh saloh^n]	*living room*

1 Are the following nouns masculine (m.) or feminine (f.)?

noun *(nom)*	m.	f.
mère		
chambre		
fils		
salon		
grenier		
maison		

2 Unscramble the letters of these words for rooms and then write the English equivalent.

a. naols = ... = ...

b. iosman = ... = ...

c. ggaare = ... = ...

d. iieunsc = ... = ...

e. mbhraec = ... = ...

f. eeirgrn = ... = ...

Singular and plural nouns *(Les noms singuliers et pluriels)*

- To form the plural, either an **s** is added (**une fille** *a girl* → **des filles** *some girls*), or sometimes an **x** or **ux** (**un cheveu** *a hair* → **des cheveux** *some hair*, **un journal** *a newspaper* → **des journaux** *some newspapers*).
- If a noun ends in **-s**, **-x**, or **-z**, it doesn't change in the plural (**le fils** *the son* → **les fils** *the sons*).

3 Make the following singular nouns plural, as shown in the example.

E.g. un frère = des frères

a. un grenier = des ....

b. une sœur = des ....

c. un salon = des ....

d. un parfum = ...

e. une chambre = ...

f. un père = ...

Feminine and masculine nouns: people and jobs *(Noms masculins et féminins : les personnes et les métiers)*

- Articles (*a/an, the*) also have masculine and feminine forms in French. When referring to a male, **un** or **le** is used: **un homme** *a man*, **le père** *the father*. When referring to a female, **une** or **la** is used: **une femme** *a woman*, **la mère** *the mother*.
- Often, an **-e** is added to a masculine noun to make the feminine form: **le chat** *the cat* (m.) → **la chatte** (f.).
- But some nouns undergo a more drastic change. Here are some ways masculine endings change to feminine: **-er** → **-ère**, **-en** → **-enne**, **-an** → **-anne**, **-on** → **-onne**, **-eur** → **-euse**, **-eur** → **-rice**, **-at** → **-atte**, **-f** → **-ve**, **-x** → **-se**.
- Some nouns referring to occupations can be used for either a male or a female: **professeur** *teacher* (m./f.), **un/une élève** *a student* (m./f.).

4 Who is speaking? A woman (W), a man (M) or either one (W/M)?

	W	M	W/M
a. Je suis (*I am [a]*) fermière.			
b. Je suis coiffeur.			
c. Je suis pharmacienne.			
d. Je suis professeur.			
e. Je suis secrétaire.			
f. Je suis avocat.			
g. Je suis comédien.			

Jobs and occupations *(Les métiers)*

un avocat [a^n avoka] **/ une avocate** [ewn avokat]	*a lawyer*
un boucher [booshay] **/ une bouchère** [booshehr]	*a butcher*
un boulanger [boolah^{n}jzay] **/ une boulangère** [boolah^{n}jzehr]	*a baker*
un chanteur [shah^{n}tuhr] **/ une chanteuse** [shah^{n}tuhz]	*a singer*
un coiffeur [kwafuhr] **/ une coiffeuse** [kwafuhz]	*a hairdresser*
un comédien [komaydee-a^n] **/ une comédienne** [kohmaydee-ehn]	*an actor / an actress*
un/une dentiste [dah^{n}teest]	*a dentist*
un étudiant [aytewdee-ah^n] **/ une étudiante** [aytewdee-ah^{n}t]	*a student*
un fermier [fehrmee-ay] **/ une fermière** [fehrmee-ehr]	*a farmer*
un infirmier [a^{n}feermee-ay] **/ une infirmière** [a^{n}feermee-ehr]	*a nurse*
un médecin [mayduhsa^n]	*a doctor*
un musicien [mewzeesee-a^n] **/ une musicienne** [mewzeesee-ehn]	*a musician*
un pharmacien [farmasee-a^n] **/ une pharmacienne** [farmasee-ehn]	*a pharmacist*
un professeur [profehsuhr]	*a teacher*
un/une secrétaire [suhkraytehr]	*a secretary*
un serveur [sehrvuhr] **/ une serveuse** [sehrvuhz]	*a waiter / a waitress*

5 Make the following sentences plural.

a. Je suis musicienne. Nous sommes *(We are)* ....

b. Je suis médecin. Nous sommes ....

c. Je suis dentiste. Nous sommes ....

d. Je suis bouchère. Nous sommes ....

e. Je suis chanteuse. Nous sommes ....

6 Now note whether the sentences above are masculine (m.), feminine (f.) or could be either (m./f.), as in the example.

a. Je suis musicienne. → f.

b. .... **c.** .... **d.** .... **e.** ....

7 Based on what you've learned so far, can you answer the following questions?

a. What is the French feminine indefinite article (*a, an*)? ....

b. What is the French masculine indefinite article (*a, an*)? ....

c. What is the plural form of the indefinite article (*some*)? ....

d. What is the French feminine definite article (*the*)? ....

e. What is the French masculine definite article (*the*)? ....

f. What is the plural form of the definite article? ....

g. How do you say *I am* and *We are* in French? ....

h. What is left out when saying what someone's job is in French compared to in English? ....
....
....
....

Definite articles *(Les articles définis)*

The definite article *the* has four forms in French. It needs to agree in gender and number with the word it precedes:

- **le** (masc. sing.): **le père**
- **la** (fem. sing.): **la mère**
- **l'** before a singular noun starting with a vowel or a silent **h**: **l'ami**, **l'hôtel**
- **les** (plural): **les parents** [lay parah^n]

	Singular	Plural
Masculine	**le, l'**	**les**
Feminine	**la, l'**	**les**

8 Circle the correct definite article.

a. Le / La / L' / Les maison est grande *(big)*.

b. Le / La / L' / Les enfants sont gentils *(nice)*.

c. Le / La / L' / Les salon est petit *(small)*.

d. Le / La / L' / Les garçons sont blonds.

e. Le / La / L' / Les filles sont belles *(pretty)*.

f. Le / La / L' / Les chambre est rose *(pink)*.

9 Underline the correct noun based on the definite article.

a. La **chambres / cuisine / salon** est grande.

b. Les **fille / enfant / garçons** sont gentils.

c. L' **secrétaire / avocat / fermier** est sérieux.

d. Le **comédien / chanteuse / musiciennes** est génial *(great)*.

'To be' and 'to have' ***(être et avoir)***

être [ehtr] *to be*		**avoir** [avwar] *to have*	
je suis [jzuh sew-ee]	*I am*	**j'ai** [jzay]	*I have*
tu* es [tew eh]	*you are*	**tu* as** [tew a]	*you have*
il/elle est [eel/ehl eh]	*he/she/it is*	**il/elle a** [eel/ehl a]	*he/she/it has*
nous sommes [noo som]	*we are*	**nous avons** [noo zavoh^n]	*we have*
vous êtes** [voo zeht]	*you are*	**vous** avez** [voo zavay]	*you have*
ils/elles sont [eel/ehl soh^n]	*they are*	**ils/elles ont** [eel/ehl zoh^n]	*they have*

*Informal singular **Plural *you* and also formal singular

10 Match each conjugated form of *to be* (être) with the corresponding subject pronoun.

JE	SOMMES
TU	EST
IL/ELLE	ÊTES
NOUS	SUIS
VOUS	SONT
ILS/ELLES	ES

11 Match each conjugated form of *to have* (avoir) with the corresponding subject pronoun.

J'	ONT
TU	A
IL/ELLE	AVEZ
NOUS	AI
VOUS	AS
ILS/ELLES	AVONS

Match the picture to the job. 

1. Un boucher

2. Un médecin

3. Une serveuse

a. b. c. d. e. f.

4. Un professeur

5. Une chanteuse

6. Un boulanger

Bien! You've reached the end of Lesson 3! Count up the icons for each exercise and record your results here and in the table on page 127.

Pronouns & more on articles

(indefinite/partitive articles, subject/object pronouns)

Indefinite articles *(Les articles indéfinis)*

- The French equivalents of *a/an* (used to refer to a non-specific singular noun) are **un** (before a masculine noun) and **une** (before a feminine noun): **<u>un</u> garcon** *a boy*, **<u>une</u> fille** *a girl*.
- The article **des** *some* is used in front of plural non-specific but countable nouns (both masculine and feminine): **<u>des</u> frères** *brothers*, **<u>des</u> sœurs** *sisters*.

	Singular	Plural
Masculine	**un**	**des**
Feminine	**une**	**des**

1 Circle the correct indefinite article in each sentence.

a. Il y a *(There is/are)* **un** / **une** / **des** enfants dans *(in)* la maison.

b. Il y a **un** / **une** / **des** homme dans le salon.

c. Il y a **un** / **une** / **des** chat *(male cat)* dans la chambre.

d. Il y a **un** / **une** / **des** fille dans la cuisine.

e. Il y a **un** / **une** / **des** garçon dans le grenier.

Furniture *(Le mobilier)*

un bureau [a^n bewroh]	*a desk*
un canapé [a^n kanapay]	*a sofa*
une chaise [ewn shehz]	*a chair*
un frigo [a^n freego]	*a refrigerator*
une lampe [ewn lah^{n}p]	*a lamp*
un lit [a^n lee]	*a bed*
une table [ewn tabl]	*a table*
une table de nuit [ewn tabl duh new-ee]	*a nightstand, bedside table*

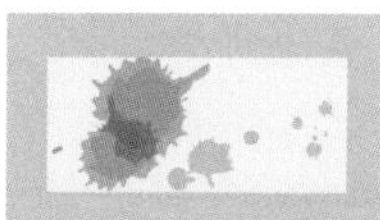

2 **Fill in the blanks using the appropriate indefinite article.**

« Dans la maison, il y a **(a)** .... cuisine avec **(b)** .... grande table et **(c)** .... chaises. Il y a trois chambres avec **(d)** .... lits confortables et **(e)** .... tables de nuit élégantes. Il y a **(f)** .... bureau et **(g)** .... toilettes. Il y a aussi *(also)* **(h)** .... petit salon avec **(i)** .... canapés. »

Partitive articles *(Les articles partitifs)*

A partitive article is used to express quantities that cannot be counted: for example, mass nouns referring to drinks or food. In English, the partitive articles *some* and *any* are often omitted, but they are ALWAYS required in French: **J'ai des amis.** *I have friends.*

There are four forms:

- **du** (m. sing.): **du café** *some coffee*
- **de la** (f. sing.): **de la salade** *some salad*
- **de l'** before a singular noun starting with a vowel or a silent **h**: **de l'eau** *some water*
- **des** (plural): **des biscuits** *some biscuits.*

	Singular	Plural
Masculine	**du, de l'**	**des**
Feminine	**de la, de l'**	**des**

Food and drinks ***(Les aliments et les boissons)***

l'ananas [lananas] (m.)	*pineapple*
la banane [la banan]	*banana*
les bonbons [lay boh^{n}boh^n]	*sweets, candy*
le café [luh kafay]	*coffee*
le concombre [luh koh^{n}koh^{n}br]	*cucumber*
l'eau [loh]	*water*
la fraise [la frehz]	*strawberry*
le fromage [luh fromajz]	*cheese*
le gâteau [luh gatoh]	*cake*
la glace [la glas]	*ice cream*
le jambon [luh jzah^{n}boh^n]	*ham*

le jus d'orange [luh jzew dorah^{n}jz] (**orange** [f.])	*orange juice*
le lait [luh leh]	*milk*
le pain [luh pa^n]	*bread*
les pâtes [lay pat]	*pasta*
le poisson [luh pwasoh^n]	*fish*
la pomme [la pom]	*apple*
la pomme de terre [la pom duh tehr]	*potato*
la salade [la salad]	*salad*
la tomate [la tomat]	*tomato*
la viande [la vee-ah^{n}d]	*meat*

Meals

In France, **le petit déjeuner** *breakfast* often consists of bread or pastries with a bowl of hot chocolate for children or coffee with milk for adults. **Le déjeuner** *lunch* can last an hour or more, and **le dîner** *dinner* is usually eaten after 7 pm.

3 **In the table below, indicate whether each partitive article is masculine (M) or feminine (F), as well as whether it is singular (S) or plural (P).**

	M	F	S	P
a. de la viande				
b. des fraises				
c. du fromage				
d. de l'ananas				
e. de l'orange				
f. des bonbons				
g. de la pomme de terre				

4 **You are at a restaurant. Complete your order using the correct partitive articles from the options below.**

de la du des de l' de la du des de la

- *Bonjour, monsieur !*

- *Bonjour. Je voudrais* (I would like) **(a)** .... *salade avec* (with) **(b)** .... *concombre et* **(c)** .... *tomates. Ensuite* (then), *je voudrais* **(d)** .... *viande avec* **(e)** .... *pommes de terre et* **(f)** .... *pain. En dessert, je voudrais* **(g)** .... *glace. Merci !*

- *Et comme boisson ?*

- *Juste* **(h)** .... *eau. Merci !*

5 Translate these phrases into French using the correct partitive article.

a. some cake ....

b. some sweets ....

c. some milk ....

d. some tomato ....

e. some meat ....

f. some pasta ....

6 Write each phrase under the correct picture.

a. du pain **b.** de la glace **c.** du poisson **d.** de la pomme **e.** de l'eau **f.** du jambon

1. .... **2.** .... **3.** .... **4.** .... **5.** .... **6.** ....

Subject pronouns *(Les pronoms sujets)*

- A pronoun is a word used in place of a noun.
- A subject pronoun refers to the person or thing performing the action of the verb: **Gaston aime les frites.** *Gaston likes chips.* → **Il aime les frites.** *He likes chips.*
- The French subject pronouns are:

Singular		Plural	
je/j'	*I*	**nous**	*we*
tu	*you* (informal)	**vous**	*you* (also used for formal sing.)
il	*he, it* (m.)	**ils**	*they* (m.)
elle	*she, it* (f.)	**elles**	*they* (f.)

- Note that **je** becomes **j'** in front of a vowel or silent **h**: **J'ai un frère.** *I have a brother.*
- French has different words for *you*. The informal singular **tu** is used when talking to a friend or family member, while **vous** is used to address someone more politely. The pronoun **vous** is also used when speaking to more than one person, in any context.
- The pronouns **il/elle** and **ils/elles** are used to refer to both people and things. These pronouns must agree in gender and number with the noun they replace.
- Note: in French, the masculine takes precedence over the feminine; which means that, if for example, you are referring to a group of people constituted of three women and one man, the subject pronouns will have to be masculine and plural (**ils**).

7 Match each French subject pronoun to its English equivalent.

elle	*I*
nous	*you* (sing.)
je/j'	*they* (m.)
ils	*we*
vous	*you* (pl.)
il	*they* (f.)
tu	*he*
elles	*she*

8 Complete the following sentences using the correct subject pronoun.

a. .... suis étudiante *(student).*

b. .... sommes acteurs *(actors).*

c. .... êtes gentils *(nice).*

d. .... sont actrices *(actresses).*

e. .... est grand *(tall,* m.*).*

f. .... ai deux lits.

Direct object pronouns (Les pronoms objets directs)

- A direct object is something that receives the action of the verb: *I call you.*
- In French, direct object pronouns are placed in front of the verb: **Louis te regarde.** *Louis is looking at you.*

Direct object pronouns	
me/m'	*me*
te/t'	*you* (informal sing.)
le/l'	*him/it* (m.)
la/l'	*her/it* (f.)
nous	*us*
vous	*you* (plural / formal)
les	*them*

Note: **m'**, **t'**, **l'** are used when in front of a vowel.

A few *-er* verbs (*Quelques verbes en -er*)

aider [ayday]	*to help*
aimer [aymay]	*to like / love*
aller [alay]	*to go*
appeler [apuhlay]	*to call*
demander [duhmah^{n}day]	*to ask*
donner [donay]	*to give*
écouter [aykootay]	*to listen*
embrasser [ah^{n}brasay]	*to kiss*
expliquer [ehkspleekay]	*to explain*
parler [parlay]	*to speak*
regarder [ruhgarday]	*to look / watch*
téléphoner [taylayfonay]	*to phone*

9 Match the French direct object pronoun to its English counterpart.

te/t'	**le/l'**	**vous**	**nous**	**me/m'**	**les**	**la/l'**
them	*you* (for. pl.)	*us*	*you* (inf. sg.)	*her/it*	*me*	*him/it*

10 Complete these sentences using the correct direct object pronoun. 

a. Il .... appelle. *(me)*
b. Nous .... aimons. *(them)*
c. Vous .... regardez. *(her)*
d. Je .... aide. *(you,* inf. sing.*)*
e. Tu .... embrasses. *(us)*
f. Elles .... écoutent. *(him)*

Indirect object pronouns *(Les pronoms objets indirects)*

An indirect object is the receiver of the direct object of the verb. They mainly occur with verbs that express giving, telling, offering or showing something to someone. Typically they indicate to or for whom something is done: **Ils te donnent le livre.** *They give the book to you.* The indirect object pronouns are:

Indirect object pronouns (sing.)	
me/m'	*to me*
te/t'	*to you* (informal)
lui	*to him*
lui	*to her*

Indirect object pronouns (pl.)	
nous	*to us*
vous	*to you* (also formal sing.)
leur	*to them*

A tip for knowing if an indirect object pronoun is required is to ask whether an action is directed 'toward' or 'at' someone (**à qui ?** *to whom?*). If so, either a preposition is needed before the noun, or an indirect object pronoun is used: **Sophie parle à Jérôme.** *Sophie speaks to Jerome.* ➜ **Sophie lui parle.** *Sophie speaks to him.*

Sophie	**parle**	**à**	**Jérôme.**
subject	verb	preposition	noun
Sophie	**lui**	**parle.**	
subject	indirect object pronoun	verb	

11 Complete these sentences using the correct indirect object pronoun. 

a. Elles .... expliquent la route. *(to me)*
b. Je .... parle. *(to you,* pl.*)*
c. Nous .... donnons du pain. *(to them)*
d. Vous .... téléphonez. *([to] her)*
e. Tu .... demandes. *([to] him)*

Great work! You've reached the end of Lesson 4! Now count up the icons for each exercise and record your results here and on page 127.

Adjectives

(agreement with nouns, word order)

Gender and number agreement *(Accord en genre et en nombre)*

- An adjective is a word used to describe an attribute of a noun or a pronoun. While an English adjective doesn't change form, a French adjective must agree with the gender (feminine or masculine) and number (singular or plural) of the noun it describes. With many adjectives, this results in four possible forms:

	Singular	Plural
Masculine	**joli** *pretty*	**jolis**
Feminine	**jolie**	**jolies**

- To form the feminine, an **-e** is usually added to the masculine form: **joli** → **jolie**.
- However, if the masculine form already ends in **e**, it does not change in the feminine: **Il est triste.** → **Elle est triste.** *He/She is sad.* Some adjectives change from the masculine to the feminine in more irregular ways: **-n** → **-nne**, **-c** → **-que**, **-l** → **-lle**, **-er** → **-ère**, **-et** → **-ète**, **-et** → **-ette**, **-eur** → **-euse**, **-eur** → **-rice**, **-f** → **-ve**, **-c/-s** → **-che**, **-g** → **-gue**, **-x** → **-se**, **-u** → **-uë**. And sometimes the feminine form of an adjective is very different from the masculine: **vieux** *old* (m.) → **vieille** (f.) or **fou** *mad, crazy* (m.)→ **folle** (f.). You'll just have to learn these as you go!
- To form the plural, usually an **-s** is added to the singular form: **joli** → **jolis**. If the singular form already ends in **-s** or **-x**, then it doesn't change. If the singular form is **-al**, this usually becomes **-aux**, and **-eau** usually becomes **-eaux**.

Some qualifying adjectives *(Quelques adjectifs qualificatifs)*

bon [boh^{n}]	*good*
drôle [drohl]	*funny*
fou [foo]	*crazy*
gentil [jzah^{n}tee]	*nice / kind*
grand [grah^{n}]	*tall / big*
heureux [uhruh]	*happy*
jeune [jzuhn]	*young*
joli [jzolee]	*pretty / attractive*

léger [lehjzay]	*light*
lourd [loor]	*heavy*
mauvais [moveh]	*bad*
méchant [mehshah^{n}]	*mean*
moche [mosh]	*ugly*
petit [puhtee]	*small*
triste [treest]	*sad*
vieux [vee-uh]	*old*

1 Write the feminine form of each of the following masculine adjectives.

a. Il est joli. → Elle est ....

b. Il est petit. → Elle est ....

c. Il est lourd. → Elle est ....

d. Il est vieux. → Elle est ....

e. Il est méchant. → Elle est ....

f. Il est jeune. → Elle est ....

2 Write the plural form of each of the following singular adjectives.

a. Il est lourd. → Ils sont ....

b. Elle est grande. → Elles sont ....

c. Il est léger. → Ils sont ....

d. Elle est triste. → Elles sont ....

e. Il est fou. → Ils sont ....

f. Elle est moche. → Elles sont ....

3 Match up the opposites.

vieille	méchantes
petits	belle
gentilles	triste
moche	jeune
heureuse	mauvais
lourde	grands
bons	légère

4 Fill in the table with the missing forms of these adjectives.

masculine singular	feminine singular	masculine plural	feminine plural
joli	jolie	a.	jolies
b.	heureuse	heureux	heureuses
grand	grande	grands	c. ....
mauvais	mauvaise	d.	mauvaises
petit	e.	petits	petites
beau *(beautiful)*	belle	beaux	f....................
bon	g.	bons	bonnes
h.	vieille	vieux	vieilles

Word order and adjectives (L'ordre des mots et des adjectifs)

- While in English adjectives come before a noun they describe, in French they are usually placed after the noun: *a blue house* → **une maison bleue**.
- Certain adjectives, however, come before the noun. These include **beau**, **bon**, **gentil**, **grand**, **jeune**, **joli**, **mauvais**, **petit**, **vieux** and the cardinal numbers.

Colours *(Les couleurs)*

blanc [blah^n]	*white*
bleu [bluh]	*blue*
gris [gree]	*grey*
jaune [jzohn]	*yellow*
marron [maroh^n]	*brown*
noir [nwar]	*black*

orange [orah^{n}jz]	*orange*
rose [roz]	*pink*
rouge [roojz]	*red*
vert [vehr]	*green*
violet [vyoleh]	*purple*

Note: Colours that take their name from fruits (**cerise** *cherry*, **olive**), flowers (**lavande**) (but **rose** and **violet** are exceptions), gems (**émeraude**) or metals (**argent** *silver*) or are in compound forms (**bleu marine** *navy blue*) do not change in the feminine or the plural: **Les chaussures sont marron.** *The shoes are brown* (**marron** *chestnut*). **Elle a des yeux bleu clair.** *She has light blue eyes.*

5 Fill in the table with the missing forms of these colours.

	masculine singular	feminine singular	masculine plural	feminine plural
	jaune	jaune	jaunes	jaunes
	1.	2.	violets	3. ....
	vert	4.	5.	6. ....
	7.	8.	9.	bleues
	10.	orange	11.	12. ....
	13.	14.	gris	15. ....
	16.	blanche	17.	18. ....
	19.	20.	21.	noires
	rouge	22.	23.	24. ....
	25.	26.	marron	27. ....
	28.	rose	29.	30. ....

6 Underline the correct form of the adjective.

a. La table est **vert / verte / verts**.

b. Les canapés sont **violet / violettes / violets**.

c. Les chaises sont **blanche / blancs / blanches**.

d. Le bureau est **noir / noire / noirs**.

e. Les tables de nuit sont **bleues / bleue / bleus**.

7 Now translate the sentences from the exercise above.

a. ....

b. ....

c. ....

d. ....

e. ....

Countries and nationalities *(Les pays et les nationalités)*

- Countries in French have a gender: **la Finlande** *Finland*.
- Nationality, which is an adjective, needs to agree with the gender of the person described: **un Australien** (m.), **une Australienne** (f.).
- When giving a person's nationality, a capital letter is used. However, if describing a quality related to a country (including language), the adjective is not capitalized (**la cuisine française; les enfants sont anglais**).

Country		**Nationality** (m. sing.)	
l'Allemagne [almany] (f.)	*Germany*	**Allemand** [aluhmah^n]	*German*
l'Angleterre [ah^{n}gluhtehr] (f.)	*England*	**Anglais** [ah^{n}gleh]	*English*
l'Australie [ohstralee] (f.)	*Australia*	**Australien** [ohstralya^n]	*Australian*
la Belgique [behljzeek] (f.)	*Belgium*	**Belge** [behljz]	*Belgian*
le Canada [kanada] (m.)	*Canada*	**Canadien** [kanadya^n]	*Canadian*
la Chine [sheen] (f.)	*China*	**Chinois** [sheenwa]	*Chinese*
l'Espagne [ehspany] (f.)	*Spain*	**Espagnol** [ehspanyol]	*Spanish*
les États-Unis [ayta zewnee] (m.)	*United States*	**Américain** [amehreeka^n]	*American*
la France [frah^{n}s] (f.)	*France*	**Français** [frah^{n}seh]	*French*
l'Italie [eetalee] (f.)	*Italy*	**Italien** [eetalya^n]	*Italian*
le Japon [jzapoh^n] (m.)	*Japan*	**Japonais** [jzaponeh]	*Japanese*
les Pays-Bas [peh-ee-ba] (m.)	*Netherlands*	**Néerlandais** [nay-ehrlah^{n}deh]	*Dutch*
la Suisse [sew-ees] (f.)	*Switzerland*	**Suisse** [sew-ees]	*Swiss*

8 Fill in the table with the missing forms of these nationalities.

flags	masc. sing.	fem. sing.	masc. pl.	fem. pl.
	Néerlandais	1.	*Néerlandais*	*Néerlandaises*
	2.	*Espagnole*	*Espagnols*	*Espagnoles*
	3.	*Italienne*	4.	*Italiennes*
	Japonais	5.	*Japonais*	6. ....
	7.	8.	9.	*Allemandes*
	Suisse	10.	11.	12. ....
	Australien	*Australienne*	13.	14. ....

9 Circle all the nationalities you can find in the word puzzle below that correspond to the list in English (all directions).

F	C	V	T	D	H	A	L	N	A
S	E	I	D	O	I	S	O	A	C
E	A	P	L	C	D	D	N	M	N
N	N	M	V	B	E	L	G	E	N
N	G	L	E	J	N	E	A	R	E
E	L	B	S	A	H	S	P	I	I
I	A	N	O	P	I	L	S	C	L
D	I	E	E	O	C	S	E	A	A
A	S	B	N	N	S	U	T	I	R
N	D	I	T	A	L	I	E	N	T
A	H	S	N	I	A	S	I	E	S
C	S	D	E	S	D	S	F	D	U
N	A	D	N	A	M	E	L	L	A

Spanish
Australian
Belgian
Chinese
Italian
Swiss
American (fem.)
English
Japanese
German
Canadian (fem.)

Well done! You've completed Lesson 5. Now count up the icons for each exercise and record your result here and in the table on page 127.

Possession & likes and dislikes

(possessive/demonstrative adjectives, expressing likes/dislikes)

Possessive adjectives *(Les adjectifs possessifs)*

A possessive adjective indicates who something belongs to (e.g. *my, your, his, her,* etc.). In French, a big difference with English is that a possessive adjective must agree in gender and number with the noun that is 'possessed' and not with the 'possessor': **sa mère** *his/her mother*, **son père** *his/her father*, **ses parents** *his/her parents.* Here are the three forms of each possessive adjective:

1 masculine object possessed		1 feminine object possessed		More than 1 object possessed	
mon	*my*	**ma**	*my*	**mes**	*my*
ton*	*your*	**ta***	*your*	**tes***	*your*
son	*his/her/its*	**sa**	*his/her/its*	**ses**	*his/her/its*
notre	*our*	**notre**	*our*	**nos**	*our*
votre**	*your*	**votre****	*your*	**vos****	*your*
leur	*their*	**leur**	*their*	**leurs**	*their*

Note: **mon, ton** and **son** are used in front of a feminine noun if it begins with a vowel or a silent **h**. For the plural form, the possessive adjective is the same for both genders.

* Informal singular ** Plural and also formal singular

Pets ***(Les animaux familiers)***

le chat [sha] / **la chatte** [shat]	*cat*
le cheval* [shuhval] / **la jument** [jzewmah^{n}]	*horse*
le chien [shya^{n}] / **la chienne** [shyehn]	*dog*
le hamster [amstehr]	*hamster*
le lapin [lapa^{n}] / **la lapine** [lapeen]	*rabbit*
le poisson [pwasoh^{n}]	*fish*
le serpent [sehrpah^{n}]	*snake*
la souris [sooree]	*mouse*
la tortue [tortew]	*tortoise / turtle*

* **cheval** has an irregular plural form: **chevaux** [shuhvoh]

1 Translate the following sentences into French as shown in the example.

E.g. It's my cat. (Louise) ➔ **C'est mon chat.**
(**mon** agrees with **chat** (masculine possession) and not with **Louise** (female possessor))

a. It's his mouse. (Thomas)
➔ C'est ....

b. It's their sister. (Jean et Caroline)
➔ C'est ....

c. It's your horse. (Audrey) (informal)
➔ ....

d. It's our grandfather. (Charline et Zoé)
➔ ....

e. It's your fish. (Simon et Julie)
➔ ....

f. They are your dogs. (Coralie et Louis)
➔ Ce sont ....

2 Underline the appropriate possessive adjective according to the noun.

a. Ce sont **mon** / **ma** / **mes** sœurs.

b. C'est **ton** / **ta** / **tes** tortue.

c. Ce sont **votre** / **vos** frères.

d. C'est **son** / **sa** / **ses** père.

e. C'est **notre** / **nos** chat.

f. C'est **leur** / **leurs** maison.

3 Unscramble the letters to form these French words for pets. Then add the correct definite article (*le* or *la*) and translate them into English.

a. oosinps = ... = ...

b. UIORSS = ... = ...

c. tnpsree = ... = ...

d. eavlhc = ... = ...

e. NAELIP = ... = ...

f. matrshe = ... = ...

Likes and dislikes *(Ce qu'on aime et ce qu'on n'aime pas)*

To express likes and dislikes in French, you can use the verbs **aimer** *to like*, **adorer** *to love* or **détester** *to hate*. All three are regular verbs ending in **-er** and are conjugated in the present tense as shown in the table.

aimer *to like*	
j'aime	*I like*
tu aimes	*you like* (informal sing.)
il/elle aime	*he/she likes*
nous aimons	*we like*
vous aimez	*you like* (plural / form)
ils/elles aiment	*they like*

 **Use the previous table to complete the following statements.** 

a. In front of a verb starting with a vowel, the subject pronoun **je** becomes ....

b. In the present tense of verbs with an infinitive ending in **-er**, the first – and third – person singular conjugation ending is ....

c. The subject pronoun **vous** is used when talking to a .... of people or to one person in a .... way.

5 Now, following the conjugation model of the verb aimer, conjugate the verb adorer.

adorer *to love*	
a.	*I love*
b. tu	*you love* (informal)
c. il/elle	*he/she loves*
d. nous	*we love*
e. vous	*you love* (formal or pl.)
f. ils/elles	*they love*

Sports *(Les sports)*

Nouns		**Verbs**	
le cyclisme [seekleesm]	*cycling*	**faire** [fehr] **du** (de + le) **vélo**	*to ride a bike*
le football [footbohl]	*football/soccer*	**jouer** [jzoo-ay] **au** (à + le) **football**	*to play soccer*
la gymnastique [jzeemnasteek]	*gymnastics*	**faire** [fehr] **de la gymnastique**	*to do gymnastics*
le handball [ah^{n}dbal]	*handball*	**jouer** [jzoo-ay] **au handball**	*to play handball*
le jogging [djzogeeng]	*running*	**courir** [kooreer]	*to run*
le judo [jzewdo]	*judo*	**faire** [fehr] **du judo**	*to do judo*
la marche [marsh]	*walking*	**marcher** [marshay]	*to walk*
la natation [natasyoh^n]	*swimming*	**nager** [najzay]	*to swim*
le rugby [rewgbee]	*rugby*	**jouer** [jzoo-ay] **au rugby**	*to play rugby*
le tennis [tehnees]	tennis	**jouer** [jzoo-ay] **au tennis**	*to play tennis*

Le coq

The Gallic rooster (**coq**) is an unofficial national symbol of France and is often used as a French logo in sports such as football and rugby.

6 **Find the French translations of this list of sports in the grid (left to right and downwards).**

F	R	O	P	S	H	Y	U	F	P	M
Y	J	E	M	N	J	U	D	O	U	i
K	L	N	A	T	A	T	i	O	N	M
A	W	F	R	R	T	E	O	T	A	A
i	R	A	C	Q	E	P	O	B	T	S
S	U	T	H	A	N	D	B	A	L	L
S	G	U	E	E	N	R	T	L	J	i
H	B	M	D	S	i	Y	G	L	D	L
C	Y	C	L	i	S	M	E	B	H	M

walking
handball
football
rugby
cycling
swimming
judo

7 **Translate these sentences into English.**

a. Julien adore jouer au tennis. ➜ ....

b. Coralie et Sidonie détestent le football. ➜ ....

c. Nous aimons courir. ➜ ....

d. Vous adorez faire de la gymnastique. ➜ ....

e. Ils aiment jouer au handball. ➜ ....

8 **Use each prompt below to construct two complete sentences, as in the example.**
☺ aimer ☺☺ adorer ☹ détester

E.g. Julie ☺ soccer ➜ **Julie aime le football. / Julie aime jouer au football.**

a. We ☹ rugby ➜ Nous ....
Nous ....

b. Karine and Lucie ☺☺ swimming ➜ Karine et Lucie ....
Karine et Lucie ....

c. You ☺ cycling ➜ Tu ....
Tu ....

d. I ☹ judo ➜ Je ....
Je ....

e. You ☺☺ walking ➜ Vous ....
Vous ....

I don't like ... *(Je n'aime pas...)*

Look at the following sentences:

a) **J'aime les pâtes.** *I like pasta.*

b) **Je n'aime pas les pâtes.** *I don't like pasta.*

c) **Il regarde un film.** *He is watching a movie.*

d) **Il ne regarde pas un film.** *He is not watching a movie.*

9 Use your observations to answer the following questions.

a. Which two sentences are affirmative? ....

b. Which two sentences are negative? ....

c. What do you add to form the negative? ....

d. What difference do you notice in the negation in sentences b and d? ....

....

....

10 Rewrite the following affirmative statements as negative sentences.

a. J'aime les bonbons. ➜ ....

b. J'écoute ta mère. ➜ ....

c. Il parle beaucoup *(a lot)*. ➜ ....

d. Elles regardent la télévision. ➜ ....

e. Vous aidez votre sœur. ➜ ....

Demonstrative adjectives *(Les adjectifs démonstratifs)*

- Demonstrative adjectives are used to point out someone or something. In French they must agree in gender and number with the noun they describe:

	Singular		Plural	
Masculine	**ce, cet**	*this*	**ces**	*these*
Feminine	**cette**	*this*	**ces**	*these*

- Note: **cet** is used in front of a masculine singular noun or adjective beginning with a vowel or a silent **h**: **cet ananas** *this pineapple*, **cet homme** *this man.*

Clothes *(Les vêtements)*

la casquette [kaskeht]	*cap*
le chapeau* [shapoh]	*hat*
les chaussettes [shohseht]	*socks*
les chaussures [shohsewr]	*shoes*
la chemise [shuhmeez]	*shirt*
le chemisier [shuhmeezee-ay]	*blouse*
la jupe [jzewp]	*skirt*
le manteau* [mah^{n}toh]	*coat*
le pantalon** [pah^{n}taloh^{n}]	*trousers*
le pull-over [pewlovehr]	*jumper / sweater*
le pyjama** [peejzama]	*pyjamas*
la robe [rob]	*dress*
le tee-shirt [teeshuhrt]	*T-shirt*

* The plural forms of **chapeau** *hat* and **manteau** *coat* are **chapeaux** and **manteaux**.
** In French, both **pantalon** *trousers* and **pyjama** *pyjamas* are singular.

11 Label each picture with the corresponding word from the suitcase.

a. ....

b. ....

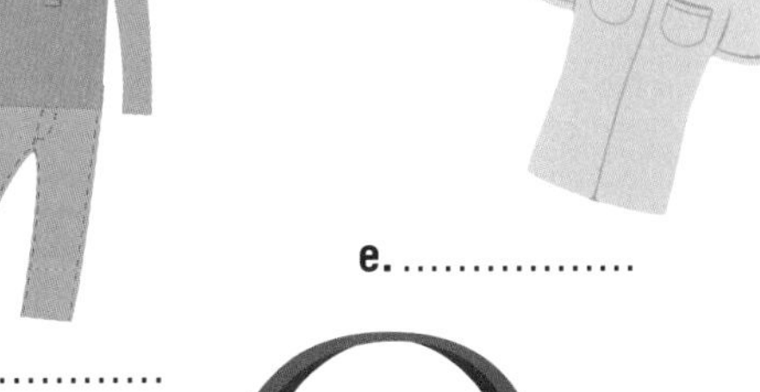

c. ....

d. ....

e. ....

12 Circle the correct demonstrative adjective.

a. **Ce / Cet / Cette / Ces** chaussettes sont rouges.

b. **Ce / Cet / Cette / Ces** chemise est blanche.

c. **Ce / Cet / Cette / Ces** pull-over est gris.

d. **Ce / Cet / Cette / Ces** pantalon est noir et jaune.

e. **Ce / Cet / Cette / Ces** casquette est bleue.

Super! You've completed Lesson 6! It's time to count up the icons for the exercises and record your result here and in the table on page 127.

7 The present tense
(regular -er/-ir/-re verbs)

The present tense of regular -er verbs *(Les verbes en -er réguliers au présent)*

- The present tense is used to talk about an action or state in the present, habitual actions and general truths. In French, it is also frequently used to talk about something that will happen in the near future. Note that in French the present tense is typically used to express the equivalent of the present continuous in English (e.g. **je regarde** *I watch* or *I am watching*).
- French verbs are categorized in three main verb groups: verbs with an infinitive ending in **-er** (1st group); verbs with an infinitive ending in **-ir** (2nd group); and verbs with an infinitive ending in **-re, -ir** and **-oir** (3rd group) (many of these are irregular verbs).
- The present tense of regular **-er** verbs is formed by replacing the infinitive ending with the conjugation endings shown in the table below.

regarder *to look / to watch*			
je regarde	*I look*	**nous regardons**	*we look*
tu regardes	*you look* (informal)	**vous regardez**	*you look* (form., pl.)
il/elle regarde	*he/she looks*	**ils/elles regardent**	*they look*

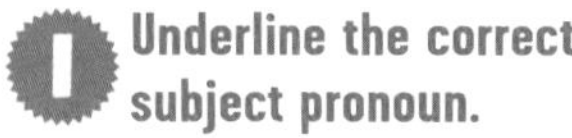

1 Underline the correct subject pronoun.

a. **J' / Tu / Ils** aime les pâtes.

b. **Il / Nous / Vous** jouez au rugby.

c. **Il / Nous / Elles** embrassent les garçons.

d. **Je / Nous / Vous** adorons la soupe.

e. **Tu / Elle / Vous** écoutes de la musique.

2 Underline the correct conjugated verb.

a. Je **regarde / regardes / regardons** le match.

b. Nous **joue / joue / jouons** au basketball.

c. Elle **téléphone / téléphonons / téléphonez** à son grand-père.

d. Vous **aides / aidez / aident** Anne-Sophie.

e. Ils **appelles / appelle / appellent** leur ami.

3 Conjugate each verb in the correct person of the present tense.

a. Tu (**parler**) .... avec *(with)* Margot.

b. Elle (**jouer**) .... au tennis.

c. Nous (**aimer**) .... courir.

d. Ils (**regarder**) .... les lions au zoo.

e. Vous (**demander**) .... de l'eau.

f. J'(**écouter**) .... mon professeur.

The present tense of regular -ir verbs *(Les verbes en -ir réguliers au présent)*

The present tense of regular **-ir** verbs is formed by replacing the infinitive ending with the conjugation endings shown here.

finir *to finish*			
je	**finis**	**nous**	**finissons**
tu	**finis**	**vous**	**finissez**
il/elle	**finit**	**ils/elles**	**finissent**

Some regular -ir verbs *(Verbes réguliers en -ir)*

agir [ajzeer]	*to act*
bâtir [bateer]	*to build*
choisir [shwazeer]	*to choose*
définir [dayfeeneer]	*to define*
finir [feeneer]	*to finish*
nourrir [nooreer]	*to feed*
réfléchir [rayflehsheer] **+ à**	*to think*
remplir [rah^{n}pleer]	*to fill*
réussir [ray-ewseer]	*to succeed*

 **Underline the correct verb form.** 

a. Il **finis / finit / finissez** son gâteau.

b. Nous **bâtis / bâtissons / bâtissez** une grande maison.

c. Vous **choisissons / choisissez / choisissent** un nouveau chien.

d. Tu **réussis / réussit / réussissons** ton examen.

e. Elles **nourrissons / nourrissez / nourrissent** les poissons.

f. Je **réfléchis / réfléchit / réfléchissez** à un cadeau *(a present)* pour Rachid.

 **Conjugate the verbs in the present tense.** 

a. Tu (**choisir**) .... un chapeau.

b. Vous (**finir**) .... votre petit déjeuner.

c. Je (**nourrir**) .... le petit frère d'Amandine.

d. Ils (**remplir**) .... les verres *(the glasses)* de leurs amis.

e. Nous (**réfléchir**) .... aux vacances *(the holidays)*.

6 Fill in the missing words by conjugating the appropriate verbs from the list.

choisir – réfléchir – remplir – finir – réussir

« Allô, Théodore ? Je **(a.)** .... le cadeau pour Marina.
Et vous ? Vous **(b.)** .... le gâteau ?

– Oui, Antoine **(c.)** .... les verres et les ballons sont sur la table.

– Super ! Nous **(d.)** .... cette surprise, d'accord *(OK)* ?
Où sont Thomas et Emma ?

– Ils **(e.)** .... à la musique pour la fête.

– Très bien. À bientôt ! »

The present tense of regular -re verbs *(Les verbes en -re réguliers au présent)*

The present tense of regular **-re** verbs is formed by replacing the infinitive ending with the conjugation endings shown here.

vendre *to sell*	
je	**vends**
tu	**vends**
il/elle	**vend**
nous	**vendons**
vous	**vendez**
ils/elles	**vendent**

Some regular -re verbs
(Verbes réguliers en -re)

attendre [atah^{n}dr]	*to wait*
descendre [dehsah^{n}dr]	*to get down / to get off*
entendre [ah^{n}tah^{n}dr]	*to hear*
rendre [rah^{n}dr]	*to give back*
répondre [raypoh^{n}dr] **+ à**	*to answer / to reply to*
perdre [pehrdr]	*to lose*
vendre [vah^{n}dr]	*to sell*

7 Complete the sentences with the appropriate subject pronoun (some have two possibilities).

a. .... vends des salades.

b. .... entendons notre chien.

c. .... répondez à la lettre de Fabrice.

d. .... attendent le bus.

e. .... descend à la cave *(the cellar)*.

8 Match up the two parts of each sentence.

1. J'entends...	**a.** ... le taxi pour l'aéroport.
2. Nous attendons...	**b.** ... à leur professeur.
3. Vous descendez...	**c.** ... ton livre à Karim.
4. Tu vends...	**d.** ... ses clés *(her keys)* dans le bus.
5. Elle perd...	**e.** ... un oiseau chanter *(sing)*.
6. Ils répondent...	**f.** ... du bus.

9 Translate these sentences into English.

a. Ils vendent leur maison. → ....

b. Nous réussissons notre gâteau. → ....

c. Vous choisissez un nom pour le chat. → ....

d. Je perds mes livres. → ....

e. Elle embrasse Pacôme. → ....

f. Tu aides Romain. → ....

10 Translate these sentences into French.

a. They finish dinner. → ....

b. I succeed at swimming. → ....

c. We get off the horse. → ....

d. She hears the dog. → ....

e. You *(informal)* give your coat. → ....

f. You *(plural)* ask for a table. → ....

Très bien! You've reached the end of Lesson 7. It's time to count up the icons for the exercises and record your result here and in the table on page 127.

63

Numbers & time

(cardinal and ordinal numbers, telling the time)

Cardinal numbers *(Les nombres cardinaux)*

- Cardinal numbers are the numbers used to count (e.g. 1, 2, 3, etc.). They answer the question **Combien de... ?** *How many?*
- The only cardinal number with a different form in the masculine and feminine is **un** *one*: **un chapeau** *one hat*, **une jupe** *one skirt*.

The numbers from 30 *(Les nombres à partir de 30)*

(See page 6 for 0–10, and page 10 for 11–29.)

30	**trente** [trah^{n}t]	78	**soixante-dix-huit**
31	**trente et un**	79	**soixante-dix-neuf**
32	**trente-deux**	80	**quatre-vingts**
40	**quarante** [karah^{n}t]	81	**quatre-vingt-un**
41	**quarante et un**	82	**quatre-vingt-deux**
42	**quarante-deux**	90	**quatre-vingt-dix**
50	**cinquante** [sa^{n}kah^{n}t]	91	**quatre-vingt-onze**
51	**cinquante et un**	92	**quatre-vingt-douze**
52	**cinquante-deux**	100	**cent** [sah^{n}]
60	**soixante** [swasah^{n}t]	101	**cent un**
61	**soixante et un**	102	**cent deux**
62	**soixante-deux**	200	**deux cents**
70	**soixante-dix**	201	**deux cent un**
71	**soixante et onze**	202	**deux cent deux**
72	**soixante-douze**	1000	**mille** [meel]
73	**soixante-treize**	2000	**deux mille**
74	**soixante-quatorze**	2001	**deux mille un**
75	**soixante-quinze**	2002	**deux mille deux**
76	**soixante-seize**	100 000	**cent mille**
77	**soixante-dix-sept**	1 000 000	**un million** [meelyoh^{n}]

Note: **vingt** and **cent** take an **s** when used after a number, unless they are followed by another number: **quatre-vingts** *80* → **quatre-vingt-treize** *93*; **deux cents** *200* → **deux cent cinquante** *250*. The number **mille** *1000* never takes an **s**.

1 Write out the numbers below in French and then find the words in the grid (in any direction).

0 = ... 13 = ... 52 = ...

3 = ... 14 = ... 64 = ...

7 = ... 15 = ... 70 = ...

8 = ... 22 = ... 81 = ...

9 = ... 30 = ... 100 = ...

10 = ... 40 = ... 1 000 = ...

12 = ... 50 = ...

E	R	T	A	U	Q	E	T	N	A	X	I	O	S
Q	D	R	C	E	Q	U	A	R	A	N	T	E	K
H	V	V	E	N	Q	O	U	D	R	L	E	T	M
A	C	I	N	Q	U	A	N	T	E	D	E	U	X
E	J	N	T	F	I	O	U	M	R	S	A	I	S
T	N	G	T	I	N	M	S	I	T	O	X	M	K
P	M	T	U	E	Z	I	E	R	T	Z	I	W	P
E	S	D	S	R	E	L	Y	A	C	J	S	S	O
S	O	E	B	O	T	L	R	M	I	I	G	G	R
F	Q	U	A	T	R	E	V	I	N	G	T	U	N
D	I	X	G	Z	E	C	X	U	Q	Y	A	C	T
O	A	F	U	E	N	A	P	D	U	A	O	V	M
U	R	H	U	I	T	T	O	B	A	Z	E	R	O
Z	U	I	S	K	E	R	I	F	N	R	U	S	O
E	B	O	M	A	Z	Q	U	A	T	O	R	Z	E
I	U	S	O	I	X	A	N	T	E	D	I	X	A

2 Write the number that comes next in the pattern.

a. zéro, trois, six, neuf, ...

b. six, douze, dix-huit, vingt-quatre, ...

c. cent, quatre-vingt-dix, quatre-vingts, ...

d. un, onze, vingt et un, trente et un, ...

e. neuf, dix-huit, vingt-sept, trente-six, ...

f. dix, douze, vingt, vingt-deux, trente, ...

3 Unscramble the letters to form numbers between 0 and 1000, adding a hyphen where necessary.

a. eaarnutetpqs = ...

b. xgdvtniue = ...

c. iellm = ...

d. usqvngttaeir = ...

e. erotuzaq = ...

f. nisxateo = ...

Ordinal numbers *(Les nombres ordinaux)*

Ordinal numbers show order, rank or position (e.g. *first, second, third*, etc.).

The only ordinal number with a feminine form is **premier** (m.) → **première** (f.).
(The final **e** is silent in the ordinal numbers in the table.)

1er / 1re	premier / première	18e	dix-huitième
2e	deuxième	19e	dix-neuvième
3e	troisième	20e	vingtième
4e	quatrième	21e	vingt et unième
5e	cinquième	22e	vingt-deuxième
6e	sixième	23e	vingt-troisième
7e	septième	24e	vingt-quatrième
8e	huitième	25e	vingt-cinquième
9e	neuvième	26e	vingt-sixième
10e	dixième	27e	vingt-septième
11e	onzième	28e	vingt-huitième
12e	douzième	29e	vingt-neuvième
13e	treizième	30e	trentième
14e	quatorzième	40e	quarantième
15e	quinzième	70e	soixante-dixième
16e	seizième	100e	centième
17e	dix-septième	1000e	millième

4 Write these ordinal numbers in digits.

E.g. quarante-quatrième = 44e

a. troisième = ...

b. millième = ...

c. soixante-dixième = ...

d. seizième = ...

e. soixantième = ...

f. dix-neuvième = ...

g. quatre-vingt-onzième = ...

5 Translate these ordinal numbers into French.

a. first =..

b. fourteenth = ...

c. twentieth = ...

d. thirty-second = ...

e. fifty-fifth = ...

f. sixty-eighth = ...

g. eighty-sixth = ...

h. hundredth = ...

6 Rewrite these cardinal numbers as ordinal numbers.

a. un = ...

b. douze =.......................................

c. cinquante = ...

d. cent = ...

e. dix-sept = ...

f. neuf = ...

g. cinquante-deux = ...

....

What time is it? *(Quelle heure est-il ?)*

- When giving the time, the French term is **heure** (f.) *hour*. While in English, the term *o'clock* can be omitted, **heure(s)** must be used with a specific time: **Il est une heure.** *It's 1:00.* **Il est six heures.** *It's 6:00.*
- In France, the 24-hour clock is commonly used: **15:15 quinze heures quinze** *3:15 p.m.* (Note that the terms **et quart** *quarter past* and **et demie** *half past* cannot be used with the 24-hour clock.)
- When using the 12-hour clock, a.m. and p.m. can be expressed with **du matin** *in the morning*, **de l'après-midi** *in the afternoon* (until 6 p.m.) or **du soir** *in the evening* (after 6 p.m.).

Giving the time *(Dire l'heure)*

Il est ...	*It is ...*
... midi. [meedee]	*... midday / noon.*
... minuit. [meenew-ee]	*... midnight.*
... une heure.	*... one o'clock.*
... deux heures.	*... two o'clock.*
... trois heures et quart.	*... a quarter past three.*
... quatre heures et demie.	*... half past four.*
... cinq heures moins le quart.	*... a quarter to five.*
... six heures dix.	*... ten past six.*
... sept heures moins vingt.	*... twenty to seven.*
un quart d'heure	*a quarter of an hour*
une demi-heure	*a half hour*
à huit heures du matin	*at eight in the morning*
à cinq heures de l'après-midi	*at five in the afternoon*
à neuf heures du soir	*at nine in the evening*

The 24-hour clock

In France, **l'heure officielle** *official time* is given with the 24-hour clock. You'll see (and hear) it in transport timetables, events schedules, programmes, and all sorts of public announcements.

Draw the time on the clocks.

a. Il est huit heures.

b. Il est seize heures.

c. Il est trois heures et demie.

d. Il est deux heures et quart.

e. Il est minuit.

f. Il est neuf heures moins le quart.

Write the time in French (in words!).

a. *Il est* .... b. .... c. .... d. .... e. .... f. ....

....

....

Match up each clock with the correct time.

08:40

22:25

06:50

neuf heures moins vingt
midi
quatre heures moins le quart
sept heures moins dix
dix heures vingt-cinq
cinq heures dix

Excellent! You've completed Lesson 8! It's now time to count up the icons for the exercises and record your result here and in the table on page 127.

9

More on the present tense

(irregular -er/-ir/-re verbs)

The present tense of irregular -er verbs *(Les verbes en -er irréguliers au présent)*

- The good news is that **aller** *to go* is the only true irregular **-er** verb: some of its present tense forms are completely different from the infinitive. However, certain spelling changes can occur in the stem of other **-er** verbs.
- Verbs with spelling changes in the first-person plural (**nous**):
  - In verbs ending in **-cer**, the **c → ç**: **nous remplaçons** *we replace.*
  - In verbs ending in **-ger**, an **e** is added to the stem: **nous rangeons** *we tidy.*
- Verbs with spelling changes in all persons except the first- and second-person plural (**nous** and **vous**): i.e. the spelling changes in the conjugations **je, tu, il/elle, ils/elles.**
  - verbs such as **acheter**: **e → è = j'achète**
  - verbs such as **nettoyer**: **y → i = tu nettoies**
  - verbs such as **appeler**: **l → ll = elle appelle**
  - verbs such as **espérer**: **é → è = elles espèrent**

Some irregular -er verbs *(Quelques verbes irréguliers en -er)*

acheter [ashuhtay]	*to buy*
aller [alay]	*to go*
appeler [apuhlay]	*to call*
envoyer [ah^{n}vwa-ee-ay]	*to send*
espérer [ehspayray]	*to hope*
jeter [jzuhtay]	*to throw*
manger [mah^{n}jzay]	*to eat*
nettoyer [netwa-ee-ay]	*to clean*
préférer [prayfehray]	*to prefer*
ranger [rah^{n}jzay]	*to tidy / to put away*

1 Underline the correct spelling of each verb.

a. Nous **espérons / espèrons** manger des pâtes.

b. Tu **achétes / achètes** des poissons.

c. Vous **commencez / commen**[…] le piano.

d. Elles **envoyent / envoient** une lettre à Sophie.

e. Nous **rangons / rangeons** la chambre de Catherine.

 **Conjugate these irregular verbs following the rules on the previous page.** 

a. Nous (**manger**) .... une délicieuse pizza !

b. Il (**jeter**) .... ses vieilles chaussettes.

c. Elles (**préférer**) .... les films drôles *(funny)*.

d. Tu (**appeler**) .... ton chien.

e. Je (**nettoyer**) .... les toilettes.

 **Match up each verb with the corresponding picture.** 

appeler | jeter | manger | acheter | envoyer | nettoyer

a.

b.

c.

d.

e.

f.

Some irregular -ir/-re/-oir verbs *(Quelques verbes irréguliers en -ir/-re/-oir)*

avoir [avwar]	*to have*
battre [batr]	*to beat*
boire [bwar]	*to drink*
craindre [kra^{n}dr]	*to fear*
croire [krwar]	*to believe*
devoir [duhvwar]	*to have to*
dire [deer]	*to say*
faire [fehr]	*to do / make*
lire [leer]	*to read*

mettre [mehtr]	*to put*
peindre [pa^{n}dr]	*to paint*
pouvoir [poovwar]	*to be able to*
prendre [prah^{n}dr]	*to take*
rompre [roh^{n}pr]	*to break*
savoir [savwar]	*to know*
tenir [tuhneer]	*to hold*
venir [vuhneer]	*to come*
vouloir [voolwar]	*to want*

The present tense of irregular -ir/-re/-oir verbs
(Les verbes en -ir/-re/-oir irréguliers au présent)

- There are five types of irregular **-re** verbs. Here are the models:

– **prendre: je prends, tu prends, il/elle prend, nous prenons, vous prenez, ils/elles prennent** (no **d** in the plural forms and double **n** in the 3rd-person plural)

– **battre: je bats, tu bats, il/elle bat, nous battons, vous battez, ils/elles battent** (drop one **t** in the singular forms)

– **mettre: je mets, tu mets, il/elle met, nous mettons, vous mettez, ils/elles mettent** (drop one **t** in the singular forms)

– **rompre: je romps, tu romps, il/elle rompt, nous rompons, vous rompez, ils/elles rompent** (add a **t** in the 3rd-person singular)

– Verbs ending in **-aindre** (**craindre**) and **-eindre** (**peindre**): **je crains, tu crains, il/elle craint, nous craignons, vous craignez, ils/elles craignent** (drop the **d** in all forms and add a **g** before the **n** in plural forms)

- But many irregular verbs don't follow a pattern and must be learned individually.

– **boire: je bois, tu bois, il/elle boit, nous buvons, vous buvez, ils/elles boivent**

– **croire: je crois, tu crois, il/elle croit, nous croyons, vous croyez, ils/elles croient**

– **devoir: je dois, tu dois, il/elle doit, nous devons, vous devez, ils/elles doivent**

– **dire: je dis, tu dis, il/elle dit, nous disons, vous dites, ils/elles disent**

– **faire: je fais, tu fais, il/elle fait, nous faisons, vous faites, ils/elles font**

– **lire: je lis, tu lis, il/elle lit, nous lisons, vous lisez, ils/elles lisent**

– **pouvoir: je peux, tu peux, il/elle peut, nous pouvons, vous pouvez, ils/elles peuvent**

– **savoir: je sais, tu sais, il/elle sait, nous savons, vous savez, ils/elles savent**

– **venir: je viens, tu viens, il/elle vient, nous venons, vous venez, ils/elles viennent**

– **vouloir: je veux, tu veux, il/elle veut, nous voulons, vous voulez, ils/elles veulent**

4 Match the subject pronoun to the rest of the sentence according to the conjugated verb (some have two possibilities).

1. Je ... — a. ... peignons le mur *(wall)* du salon.
2. Tu ... — b. ... dois boire de l'eau.
3. Elle ... — c. ... faites un gâteau au chocolat.
4. Nous ... — d. ... lisent beaucoup de *(a lot of)* livres.
5. Vous ... — e. ... dis au revoir à ta grand-mère.
6. Ils ... — f. ... met sa robe bleue.

5 Now translate the sentences from the previous exercise.

a. I ....

b. You (informal) ....

c. She ....

d. We ....

e. You (pl. or formal) ....

f. They (masc. or mixed gender) ....

6 Conjugate the verbs in the right person in the present tense.

a. Je (**croire**) .... les histoires *(stories)* de mon père.

b. Vous (**lire**) .... un livre très intéressant *(very interesting)*.

c. Elles (**pouvoir**) .... regarder la télé le dimanche *(on Sunday)*.

d. Nous (**savoir**) .... nos tables de multiplication.

e. Tu (**devoir**) .... écouter tes professeurs.

Reflexive verbs & pronouns *(Les verbes pronominaux et les pronoms réfléchis)*

- A reflexive verb includes a pronoun that indicates that the action is done to the subject. An example is *to hurt oneself*. However, many French verbs are reflexive that are not in English: e.g. **Nous <u>nous</u> réveillons.** *We wake up.* (from **se réveiller**).
- When conjugating a reflexive verb, the pronoun must be included. It needs to agree with the subject: **Je <u>me</u> lève.** *I get up.* ('I myself get-up'). The plural reflexive pronouns can also be used to mean *each other*.

Reflexive pronouns			
me	*myself*	**nous**	*ourselves*
te	*yourself* (informal)	**vous**	*yourself* (formal), *yourselves*
se	*himself, herself, itself, oneself*	**se**	*themselves*

- Note: **me, te, se** become **m', t', s'** before a vowel or silent **h**.

Some reflexive verbs *(Quelques verbes pronominaux)*

s'amuser [samewzay]	*to have fun*
s'appeler [sapuhlay] (+ name)	*to be called*
se brosser [suh brosay] **les dents**	*to brush one's teeth*
se coucher [suh kooshay]	*to go to bed*
se doucher [suh dooshay]	*to have a shower*
s'habiller [sabee-ay]	*to get dressed*
se laver [suh lavay]	*to wash oneself*
se lever [suh luhvay]	*to get up*
se promener [suh promuhnay]	*to go for a walk*
se réveiller [suh rayveh-ee-ay]	*to wake up*

The body *(Le corps)*

la bouche [boosh]	*mouth*
les bras [bra]	*arms*
les cheveux [shuhvuh]	*hair*
les doigts [dwa]	*fingers*
le dos [doh]	*back*
les jambes [jzah^{n}b]	*legs*
les mains [ma^n]	*hands*
le nez [nay]	*nose*
les oreilles [orehy]	*ears*
les pieds [pee-ay]	*feet*
la tête [teht]	*head*
le ventre [vah^{n}tr]	*stomach*
les yeux [zee-uh]	*eyes*

7 Underline the correct pronoun.

a. Je **me** / **te** / **se** lave les mains.

b. Elle **me** / **te** / **se** promène dans *(in)* la forêt.

c. Nous **me** / **nous** / **vous** amusons avec nos amis.

d. Tu **me** / **te** / **se** brosses les dents.

e. Vous **nous** / **vous** / **se** douchez tous les jours *(every day)*.

8 Complete the sentences using the correct reflexive pronoun from the bathtub.

a. Elle .... habille dans la chambre.

b. Nous .... réveillons à 8 heures.

c. Je .... amuse avec le chat.

d. Ils .... couchent tard *(late)*.

e. Vous .... levez dans l'après-midi.

f. Tu .... brosses les cheveux.

9 Conjugate the reflexive verbs using the correct person and reflexive pronoun.

a. Elle (**se coucher**) .... à 21 heures.

b. Nous (**se promener**) .... avec Marc et Lucie.

c. Je (**se laver**) .... les mains.

d. Ils (**s'habiller**) .... très vite (*very fast*) !

e. Tu (**se réveiller**) .... à 7 heures.

10 Unscramble the body parts, then translate them.

E.g. el zne → **le nez** → nose

a. al euhboc → .... = ...

b. sle eeolslri → .... = ...

c. sel niasm → .... = ...

d. lse exuhvce → .... = ...

e. sle msabej → .... = ...

f. el tnveer → .... = ...

C'est ça ! You've finished Lesson 9. It's time to count up the icons for the exercises and record your results here and in the table on page 127.

More on pronouns

(demonstrative, possessive, interrogative)

Demonstrative pronouns *(Les pronoms démonstratifs)*

- We saw the demonstrative adjectives **ce(t), cette** *this* and **ces** *these* on page 34. Demonstrative pronouns are used to replace a noun (and must agree with it).

	Masculine	Feminine
Singular	**celui** *the one*	**celle** *the one*
Plural	**ceux** *the ones*	**celles** *the ones*

- These pronouns are either:
  - followed by a preposition such as **à**, **de**, **dans**: **J'aime cette maison mais je n'aime pas celle de mes parents.** ('I like this house but I don't like the-one of my parents.')
  - followed by **-ci** and **-là** (see below)

	Masculine	Feminine	
Singular	**celui-ci**	**celle-ci**	*this one*
	celui-là	**celle-là**	*that one*
Plural	**ceux-ci**	**celles-ci**	*these*
	ceux-là	**celles-là**	*those*

- The neutral form of **celui** is **ce** (or **c'** before a vowel). It is used in front of a relative pronoun (**ce que / ce qui**) and in the expression **c'est** *this/that is.*

- Two pronouns that do not change in number and gender are **ceci** *this* and **cela** (**ça**) *that.* **Cela n'est pas vrai.** *That's not true.*

1 Match the noun with its corresponding demonstrative pronoun.

1. les chaussettes
2. le manteau
3. la robe
4. les jupes
5. le pyjama
6. les pantalons

a. ceux
b. celui
c. celles
d. celles
e. celui
f. celle

2 **Translate the sentences below into French.**

E.g. I love these dresses, but I want that one. ➜ J'adore ces robes mais je veux celle-là.

a. I love these hats, but I want this one. ➜ ....

b. I love these socks, but I want those. ➜ ....

c. I love these shirts, but I want that one. ➜ ....

d. I love these skirts, but I want these. ➜ ....

e. I love these caps, but I want this one. ➜ ....

Possessive pronouns (*Les pronoms possessifs*)

- We saw the possessive adjectives **mon/ma/mes** *my*, **ton/ta/tes** *your*, **son/sa/ses** *his, her, its*, etc. on page 30.
- A possessive pronoun replaces a possessive adjective + noun: **ma montre** *my watch* ➜ **la mienne** *mine*. It must agree in gender and number with the noun it replaces: **mes montres** *my watches* ➜ **les miennes** *mine*.

Possessive pronouns	
le mien, la mienne les miens, les miennes	*mine*
le tien, la tienne les tiens, les tiennes	*yours* (informal singular)
le sien, la sienne les siens, les siennes	*his/hers/one's*
le nôtre, la nôtre les nôtres	*ours*
le vôtre, la vôtre, les vôtres	*yours* (plural / formal sing.)
le leur, la leur les leurs	*theirs*

Classroom objects (*Les objets de la classe*)

un bâton de colle [batoh^n duh kol]	*a glue stick*
un bureau [bewro]	*a desk*
un cahier [ka-yeh]	*a notebook*
des ciseaux [seezoh]	*scissors*
des crayons de couleur [krehyoh^n duh kooluhr]	*crayons*
un crayon à papier [krehyoh^n ah papee-ay]	*a pencil*
un feutre [fuhtr]	*a felt pen*
une gomme [gom]	*a rubber / an eraser*
un livre [leevr]	*a book*
une règle [rehgl]	*a ruler*
un stylo [steeloh]	*a pen*
un tableau [tabloh]	*a board*
une trousse [troos]	*a pencil case*

3 **Use the terms on the schoolbag to fill in the missing articles and possessive pronouns. (Beware! There is one too many!)**

a. C'est leur livre. = C'est ....

b. Ce sont ses stylos. = Ce sont ....

c. C'est votre règle. = C'est ....

d. C'est mon cahier. = C'est ....

e. C'est sa trousse. = C'est ....

f. Ce sont tes gommes. = Ce sont ....

la vôtre
les siens
le leur
la nôtre
le mien
les tiennes
la sienne

4 **Fill in the answers using the correct possessive pronoun.**

E.g. Elles sont à qui ces **chaussures** ? (je) → Ce sont **les miennes** (les chaussures).
Whose shoes are those? → They are mine.

a. Il est à qui ce stylo ? (nous) → C'est ....

b. Elle est à qui cette règle ? (tu) → C'est ....

c. Ils sont à qui ces crayons de couleur ? (vous) → Ce sont ....

d. Elles sont à qui ces gommes ? (je) → Ce sont ....

e. Il est à qui ce cahier ? (elle) → C'est ....

f. Elles sont à qui ces trousses ? (ils) → Ce sont ....

5 **Unscramble the words for the following classroom objects and then draw them.**

a. nu nâotb ed lleoc = ...

....

b. nu eaaublt = ...

c. sde xiacseu = ...

d. nu ervil = ...

e. eun meomg = ...

Interrogative pronouns *(Les pronoms interrogatifs)*

- The question word **Quel ?** *Which? What?* is followed by a noun. It must agree with the noun it refers to: **Quel jour est-il ?** *What day is it?* **Quelle heure ?** *What time?* **Quels livres ?** *Which books?* **Quelles couleurs ?** *What colours?*

	Singular	Plural
Masculine	**quel**	**quels**
Feminine	**quelle**	**quelles**

- The question word **Lequel ?** *Which one?* must also agree with the noun it refers to.

	Singular	Plural
Masculine	**lequel**	**lesquels**
Feminine	**laquelle**	**lesquelles**

- The question word **Que ?** *What?* (or **qu'** in front of a vowel) and **Qui ?** *Who?* are both followed by a verb: **Qui parle ?** *Who's talking?*

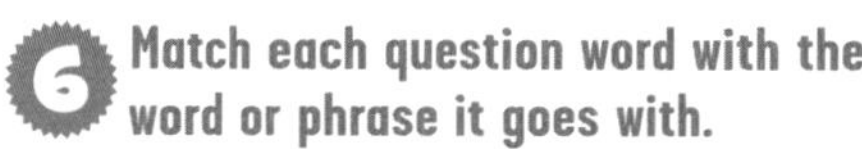

6 Match each question word with the word or phrase it goes with.

1. Quel	a. trousses ?
2. Quelle	b. veux-tu ?
3. Quels	c. livre ?
4. Quelles	d. aime les glaces ?
5. Qui	e. stylos ?
6. Que	f. chambre ?

7 Fill in the tables with the missing forms of *quel* and *lequel*.

	Singular	Plural
Masculine	**quel**	a. ....
Feminine	b.	c. ....

	Singular	Plural
Masculine	**lequel**	d. ....
Feminine	e.	f. ....

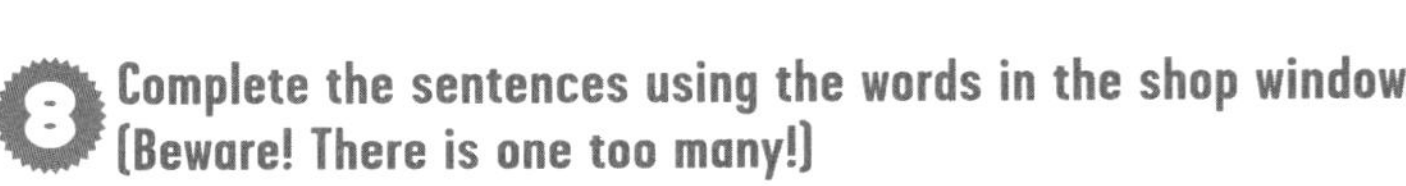

8 Complete the sentences using the words in the shop window. (Beware! There is one too many!)

E.g. **Quelle** robe aimes-tu ?

a. .... gâteau veux-tu ?

b. Regarde ces chaussures ! .... veux-tu ?

c. .... chapeaux aimes-tu ?

d. Regarde ces casquettes ! .... (sing.) aimes-tu ?

e. .... jupe veux-tu ?

f. Regarde ces pantalons ! .... aimes-tu ?

Félicitations! You've reached the end of Lesson 10. It's time to count up the icons for the exercises and record your result here and in the table on page 127.

Types of sentences
(affirmative, negative, interrogative)

The affirmative (L'affirmative)

The most common pattern in a French statement (i.e. affirmative sentence) is subject + verb + complement:

Je	**regarde**	**un film.**
subject	verb	complement

School subjects *(Les matières scolaires)*

les mathématiques [mataymateek] (fem.)	*maths*
les sciences [syah^{n}s] (fem.)	*science*
la chimie [sheemee]	*chemistry*
la géographie [jzay-ografee]	*geography*
l'histoire [eestwar] (fem.)	*history*
la littérature [leetayratewr]	*literature*
le sport [spor]	*P.E.*
la musique [mewzeek]	*music*
le français [frah^{n}seh]	*French*
l'anglais [ah^{n}gleh] (masc.)	*English*
l'informatique [a^{n}formateek] (fem.)	*I.T.*
le dessin [dehsa^n]	*art*
le théâtre [tay-atr]	*drama*

1 Put the parts of the sentences into the right column in the table.

E.g. Je mange un gâteau.

a. Il travaille dans sa chambre.

b. Nous aimons jouer au football.

c. Elle aide sa mère.

d. Vous détestez les mathématiques.

e. Tu adores l'anglais.

	Subject	Verb	Complement
	je	mange	un gâteau
a)			
b)			
c)			
d)			
e)			

2 **Put the elements into the right order to form affirmative sentences.**

E.g. suis / à Paris / je ➜ **Je suis à Paris.**

a. embrasse / elle / ton cousin ➜ ....

b. aimons / la robe bleue / nous ➜ ....

c. à votre grand-père / vous / téléphonez ➜ ....
....

d. les vacances / Loïc / en Australie / aime ➜ ....
....

e. chaussures / Carole et Clothilde / les / choisissent / rouges ➜ ....
....
....

3 **Translate the following school subjects into French using the correct article.**

a. chemistry ....

b. I.T. ....

c. French ....

d. P.E. ....

e. history..

f. art ....

The negative *(La négation)*

Some of the most common negative constructions follow the pattern **ne** + verb + one of the following:

- **pas** [pah] *not* ➜ **Nous n'avons pas de* chien.** *We don't have a dog.*

*After most negative constructions, **de** or **d'** is used instead of **un**, **une**, **des**, **du**, **de la** or **de l'**.

- **rien** [ryan] *nothing / not anything* ➜ **Je ne sais rien.** *I don't know anything.*
- **plus** [plew] *no longer / not anymore* ➜ **Solène ne joue plus.** *Solène isn't playing anymore.*
- **aucun** [ohkan] / **aucune** [ohkewn] *none / not any* ➜ **Il n'a aucun ami.** *He doesn't have any friends.*
- **jamais** [zhameh] *never* ➜ **Je ne suis jamais allé en Belgique.** *I have never been ('gone') to Belgium.*
- **ni ... ni ...** [nee] *neither ... nor ...* ➜ **Elle n'aime ni les pommes ni les poires.** *She doesn't like either apples or pears.*

Note that **ne** becomes **n'** before a vowel or a silent **h** ➜ **Il n'habite pas à Lyon.** *He doesn't live in Lyon.*

In the perfect tenses (*to have* + past participle, see page 65), the auxiliary verb **avoir** is made negative: **Il n'a jamais vu ce film.** *He has never seen this movie.*

4 **Separate the words in these sentences and add the correct punctuation.**

a. Jenaimepaslespommesvertes ....

b. Ellesnesontjamaistristes..........

c. Carlosnaaucunfilmenanglais ....

d. LouisetSuzannenejouentplusaubasketball ....
....

e. Tunesnigrandnipetit ....

5 **Translate the sentences above into English.**

a. ....

b. ....

c. ....

d. ....
....

e. ....

6 **Put the elements into the right order to form negative sentences.**

a. n' / pas / chocolat / Camille / aime / le ....

b. regarde / pas / la / Pascal / télé / ne ....

c. ai / bleu / aucun / je / chapeau / n' ....

d. mange / Ella / de / tomates / ne / jamais ....

e. ni / sœur / a / ni / n' / robe / jupe / ma ....

7 **Translate the sentences above into English.**

a. ....

b. ....

c. ....

d. ....

e. ....

The interrogative *(L'interrogation)*

Direct questions (with yes/no answers)

- Often, the word order in a question is the same as in a statement. But the subject and the verb can also be inverted. **Tu es content ?** or **Es-tu content ?** *Are you* (m.) *happy?*
- If the word order is inverted and the verb ends in a vowel while the subject starts with a vowel (**il/elle/on**), a **t** is added: **A-t-elle un chat ?** *Does she have a cat?*
- Or **est-ce que** can be put before the subject: **Est-ce que tu es content ?** *Are you happy?*

8 **Put the elements into the right order to form questions.**

a. un / tu / chat / as .... ? or .... ?

b. t / croissants / aime / les / elle .... ?

c. au / est / ils / tennis / qu' / ce / jouent .... ?

d. ce / tu / lire / que / aimes / est .... ?

e. habites / en / Italie / tu .... ? or .... ?

Question words *(Les mots interrogatifs)*

Que ?* [kuh] **Quoi ?** [kwa]	*What?*
Qui ? [kee]	*Who?*
Avec qui ? [avehk kee]	*With whom?*
Quel/quelle/quels/quelles ?** [kehl]	*Which?*
Quand ? [kah^{n}]	*When?*
Où ? [oo]	*Where?*
Pourquoi ? [poorkwa]	*Why?*
Comment ?*** [komah^{n}]	*How?*
Combien [koh^{n}bee-a^{n}] **+ de ?**	*How much? / How many?*
Combien de temps ? [koh^{n}bee-a^{n} duh tah^{n}]	*How long?*
À quelle heure ? [a kehl uhr]	*At what time?*
Est-ce que...? [ehskuh]	*Is it ...?*
Qu'est-ce que...? [kehskuh]	*What is ...?*

* **que → qu'** in front of a vowel or silent **h**.

** **quel** + masc. sing. (**Quel film ?**) / **quelle** + fem. sing. (**Quelle fille ?**) / **quels** + masc. pl. (**Quels garçons ?**) / **quelles** + fem. pl. (**Quelles maisons ?**)

*** **comment** *how* can also translate to *what*: **Comment t'appelles-tu ?** *What's your name?*

9 **Complete each question with one of the words provided. (Beware! There is one too many!) Que – Comment – Pourquoi – Qui – Où – Quand – Quelle**

a. .... viennent Lucas et Clémentine ?

b. .... manges-tu au petit déjeuner ?

c. .... chanson veux-tu *(song do you want to)* écouter ?

d. .... est le livre sur les insectes ?

e. .... préfère un fruit ?

f. .... s'appelle-t-elle ?

10 **Match up the questions and answers.**

1. *Comment vas-tu ?* •	• a. *À 13 h 35.*
2. *Pourquoi vendent-ils leur maison ?* •	• b. *Avec Émilie.*
3. *À quelle heure le train arrive-t-il ?* •	• c. *Cinq !*
4. *Avec qui Julien va-t-il au cinéma ?* •	• d. *Très bien, merci.*
5. *Combien de pantalons achètes-tu ?* •	• e. *Il est dans sa chambre.*
6. *Où est Charlie ?* •	• f. *Parce qu'ils vont habiter à (are going to live in) Paris.*

11 Translate these questions into English.

a. Qui est ce garçon ? ....

b. Pourquoi ne regarde-t-il pas ce film ? ....

c. Comment vas-tu chez Sylvain *(to Sylvain's)* demain ? ....

d. Quelle robe mets-tu pour aller à la fête *(the party)* ? ....

....

e. Quand partez-vous *(leave)* en vacances ? ....

....

f. Que mangeons-nous pour le déjeuner ? ....

12 Translate these questions into French.

a. What are you (informal sing.) listening to? ....

b. Where is Clarèle going? ....

c. Who is she? ....

d. When are you (pl.) watching the movie? ....

....

e. Why are you (informal sing.) sad? ....

Great! You've completed Lesson 11! It's time to count up the icons for the exercises and record your result here and in the table on page 127.

The past

(infinitives, past participles, the present perfect tense)

The infinitive *(L'infinitif)*

- The infinitive is the basic unconjugated form of a verb, e.g. *to love*, *to finish*, *to sell*, etc. A verb is listed in a dictionary in the infinitive.
- There are three types of infinitives in French. Each group has a specific set of conjugations in the different verb tenses, so the infinitive ending is useful for knowing which conjugation pattern to use (for regular verbs, in any case).
  - first group: -**er** ending (**aimer**)
  - second group: -**ir** ending (**finir**)
  - third group: -**re** or -**oir** ending (**vendre**, **voir**)
- To make an infinitive negative, **ne pas** is placed in front of it: **ne pas manger**.
- When two verbs are used together, the first verb is conjugated and the second is in the infinitive: **Je vais aller à l'école.** *I am going to go to school.* (Note that **aller** *to go* can be used to talk about the near future: more on this later!)
- In French, the infinitive sometimes translates to an *-ing* form in English: **J'aime lire.** *I like reading.*

The present tense of the irregular verb 'to go'
(Le verbe irrégulier « aller » au présent)

aller *to go*	
je vais [jzuh vay]	*I go/am going*
tu vas [tew va]	*you go/are going* (informal sing.)
il/elle va [eel/ehl va]	*he/she/it goes/is going*
nous allons [noo zaloh^n]	*we go/are going*
vous allez [voo zalay]	*you go/are going* (pl. / formal sing.)
ils/elles vont [eel/ehl voh^n]	*they go/are going*

1 Complete the sentences using the correct form of the verb aller.

a. Nous _______________ à la piscine *(the swimming pool)* samedi.

b. _______________ -vous chez Coraline demain matin ?

c. Elles _______________ manger des gâteaux avec Sofiane.

d. Je _______________ faire mes devoirs *(homework)* dans le salon.

e. _______________ -tu acheter le livre de Marc Levy ?

2 Write the infinitive form of the underlined verbs.

a. Ingrid regarde la télévision. ➜ ....

b. Nous avons donné un biscuit à Antoine. ➜ ....

c. J'ai fini les pommes et les bananes. ➜ ....

d. Ils sont descendus dans la cave *(the cellar)*. ➜ ....

e. Vous remplissez les verres de jus d'orange. ➜ ....

f. Astrid a répondu à la lettre de Corentin. ➜ ....

3 First, second or third verb group? Tick the right column.

	1st group	2nd group	3rd group
chanter			
apprendre			
définir			
boire			
vendre			
répondre			
nourrir			
savoir			
entendre			
ranger			
pouvoir			

4 Translate the infinitives into French, followed by their verb group.

E.g. to sing ➜ **chanter (1)**

a. to learn ➜ .... (.......)

b. to read ➜ .... (.......)

c. to eat ➜ .... (.......)

d. to come ➜ .... (.......)

e. to get up ➜ .... (.......)

f. to hope ➜ .... (.......)

g. to do ➜ .... (.......)

Past participles (*Les participes passés*)

- A past participle is the form of the verb, typically ending in *-ed* in English, used to form perfect tenses, e.g. *asked, walked*, etc. (irregular forms include *gone, brought, been*, etc.). In French, it is formed by replacing the infinitive ending with the appropriate past participle ending, according to the group the verb belongs to.
- In addition to its use in the perfect tenses (**j'ai vu** *I've seen*), a past participle can be used as an adjective: **Je suis fatigué / fatiguée.** *I'm tired.* (m./f.)
- Regular past participles are formed as follows:

	Infinitive	Ending	Drop	Add	Past participle
1st group	**aimer**	**-er**	**er**	**é**	**aimé** *loved*
2nd group	**finir**	**-ir**	**ir**	**i**	**fini** *finished*
3rd group	**vendre**	**-re**	**re**	**u**	**vendu** *sold*

- However, some verbs, such as **aller** and **faire**, are irregular.

The irregular verb 'to do/make' (*Le verbe irrégulier « faire »*)

Present tense (faire *to do, to make*)		Present perfect
je fais [jzuh feh]	*I do/am doing*	**j'ai fait** *I have done*
tu fais [tew feh]	*you do/are doing*	**tu as fait** *you have done*
il/elle fait [eel/ehl feh]	*he/she does/is doing*	**il/elle a fait** *he/she has done*
nous faisons [noo fuhzoh^n]	*we do/are doing*	**nous avons fait** *we have done*
vous faites [voo feht]	*you do/are doing*	**vous avez fait** *you have done*
ils/elles font [eel/ehl foh^n]	*they do/are doing*	**ils/elles ont fait** *they have done*

5 **Fill in the table with the infinitive and regular past participle for each verb.**

Present tense	Infinitive	Past participle
Elle déteste les oranges.		
Nous perdons toujours nos clés *(keys)*.		
Karine lit des livres de science-fiction.		
Nous finissons nos devoirs.		
Aimes-tu les crêpes ?		
Lucien réussit ses examens.		

6 Unscramble these verbs in the present perfect (see below) and translate them.

E.g. i'aj arépl → j'ai parlé → I talked/I spoke

a. UT SA UETANTD → .... → ....

b. uson snoav érregad → .... → ....

c. UOVS ZEAV NUEVD → .... → ....

d. Isi tno âitb → .... → ....

e. IAJ' PRNDUÉO → .... → ....

f. Ilee a itaf → .... → ....

The present perfect *(Le passé composé)*

In French, the present perfect is used to talk about a fully completed action or event that occurred in the past at a specific time. In English, it often translates to the simple past. It is formed with the auxiliary verb **avoir** conjugated in the present tense, followed by the past participle of the main verb (see the example for **faire** on page 64): **Il a plu vendredi dernier.** *It rained last Friday.* However, some verbs take **être** as the auxiliary verb.

Verbs that take *être* in the perfect tenses

- In the present perfect of verbs that use **être** as the auxiliary verb, the past participle must agree with the subject of the verb: **Ils sont rentrés hier.** *They came back yesterday.*
- Only certain verbs take **être** as an auxiliary. These include reflexive verbs and verbs of movement and transition. One way to remember them is with the mnemonic **DR & MRS P. VANDERTRAMP**:

devenir *to become* **(devenu), revenir** *to come back* **(revenu), monter** *to climb* **(monté), retourner** *to return* **(retourné), sortir** *to leave* **(sorti), passer** *to pass* **(passé), venir** *to come* **(venu), arriver** *to arrive* **(arrivé), naître** *to be born* **(né), descendre** *to descend* **(descendu), entrer** *to enter* **(entré), rester** *to stay* **(resté), tomber** *to fall* **(tombé), rentrer** *to come back* **(rentré), aller** *to go* **(allé), mourir** *to die* **(mort), partir** *to leave* **(parti)**

Agreement with 'to be' and 'to have' *(L'accord avec être et avoir)*

As we've seen, the present perfect is formed with a conjugated auxiliary verb followed by a past participle: **Il a réservé une chambre.** *He (has) reserved a room.* The past participle only changes form in certain specific cases.

- When **avoir** is used as the auxiliary, the past participle needs to agree with the direct object only when the latter comes before the verb: **J'ai envoyé la lettre hier.** → **Je l'ai envoyée hier.** Otherwise the past participle does not change form.
- With **être**, the past participle must agree with the subject in gender and number: **Elle est allée au théâtre.** → **Elles sont allées au théâtre.**

7 Underline the correct form of the past participle.

a. Elles ont **jeté / jetés / jetées** les papiers.

b. Nous avons **envoyé / envoyés / envoyées** une lettre à Carla.

c. Ils sont **resté / restés / restées** chez *(at)* Jean-Paul.

d. Tu as **lu / lus / lues** tous les livres.

e. Elle est **tombé / tombée / tombées** dans les escaliers *(the stairs)*.

f. Vous avez **espéré / espérés / espérées** voir vos amies.

8 Choose the right auxiliary (avoir or être) and conjugate it to form the present perfect.

a. Je .... montée dans la chambre.

b. Nous .... aimé ce restaurant.

c. Elles .... entrées dans l'école.

d. Tu .... appelé ton grand-père ?

e. Il .... voulu aller en Australie.

f. Nous .... arrivés à 10 h 30.

9 Conjugate these verbs in the present perfect.

a. Nous (**FINIR**) .... une nouvelle leçon.

b. Elle (**vouloir**) .... rentrer à la maison.

c. Vous (**faire**) .... vos lits ?

d. Elle (**aller**) .... à la banque avec sa mère.

e. Ils (**PARTIR**) .... très tôt *(very early)* ce matin.

f. J' (**vendre**) .... mon pull *(sweater)* jaune.

Irregular past participles (Participes passés irréguliers)

Most irregular verbs have an irregular past participle. Nonetheless, the endings of these past participles follow patterns:

- ending in **-u** as in **boire → bu** *drunk*, **croire → cru** *believed*, **pouvoir → pu** *could, was able*, **savoir → su** *known*
- ending in **-is** as in **mettre → mis** *put*, **prendre → pris** *taken*
- ending in **-t** as in **dire → dit** *said*, **écrire → écrit** *written*
- all others as in **être → été** *been*, **faire → fait** *done*, **offrir → offert** *offered.*

More verbs *(Verbes supplémentaires)*

comprendre [koh^{n}prah^{n}dr]	*to understand*
écrire [aykreer]	*to write*
offrir [ofreer]	*to offer*
savoir [savwar]	*to know*
voir [vwar]	*to see*

10 Complete the sentences with the appropriate past participle.

a. J'ai (comprendre) .... la leçon de maths !

b. Nous avons (boire) .... beaucoup d'eau hier *(yesterday).*

c. Sophia et Amina ont (lire) .... tous les livres de la bibliothèque *(library).*

d. As-tu (faire) .... tes devoirs ?

e. Karine a (pouvoir) .... rentrer avant 21 h.

f. Rose a (écrire) .... une longue lettre à son amie.

Well done! You've reached the end of Lesson 12! It's time to count up the icons for the exercises and record your results here and in the table on page 127.

Talking about time & weather

(prepositions and adverbs)

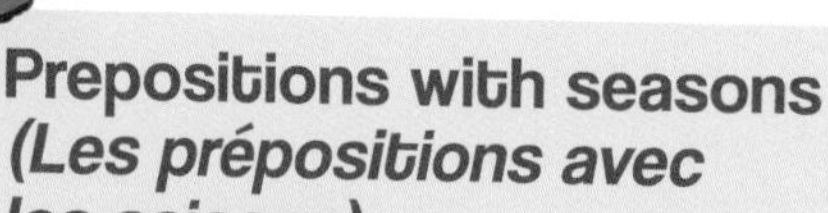

Prepositions with seasons *(Les prépositions avec les saisons)*

Observe the difference between:
Je vais à la plage en été.
I go to the beach in the summer.
Les oiseaux chantent au printemps. *The birds sing in the spring.*

en	au
en été **en hiver** **en automne**	**au printemps**

The seasons *(Les saisons)*

le printemps [pra^{n}tah^n]	*spring*
l'été [aytay]	*summer*
l'automne [ohton]	*autumn/fall*
l'hiver [eevehr]	*winter*

The four seasons are masculine in French. As mentioned in the panel on the left, the seasons are used with the preposition **en**, with the exception of **au printemps** *in the spring.*

1 Translate these sentences into French.

a. I don't go to school in the summer. → ....
....

b. Loïc is going to Portugal in the autumn. → ....
....

c. Christmas is in the winter. → ....
....

d. Cora likes eating ice cream **(des glaces)** in the spring. → ....
....

The weather *(Le temps)*

The word for *weather* is the same as for *time*: **le temps**. In French, the verb **faire** *to do/ make* rather than *to be* is used to talk about the weather: **Il fait mauvais.** ('It makes bad.') *The weather is bad.* With nouns (such as **neige** *snow*, **pluie** *rain*, **vent** *wind*), the phrase **il y a** *there is* is used: **Il y a du vent.** *It's windy.* **Il y a de la neige.** *It's snowy.* Here are some useful expressions for talking about the weather.

Quel temps fait-il?	*What's the weather like?*
Il fait beau.	*The weather is nice.*
Il fait/Il y a du vent.	*It is windy.*
Il fait mauvais.	*The weather is bad.*
Il fait froid.	*It is cold.*
Il fait chaud.	*It is hot.*

Il gèle. *[eel jzehl]*	*It is freezing.*
Il neige. [eel nehjz]	*It is snowing.*
Il pleut. [eel pluh]	*It is raining.*
l'éclair (m.) [layklehr]	*lightning*
la neige [la nehjz]	*snow*
les nuages (m.) [lay new-ajz]	*clouds*
l'orage (m.) [lorajz]	*storm*
la pluie [la plew-ee]	*rain*
le soleil [luh soleh-ee]	*sun*
le vent [luh vah^{n}]	*wind*

2 Match the correct verb phrase to each weather term.

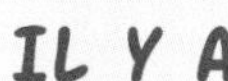

IL Y A

IL FAIT

A. ... MAUVAIS
B. ... DU SOLEIL
C. ... DU VENT
D. ... BEAU
E. ... CHAUD
F. ... DE LA PLUIE
G. ... FROID
H. ... DES NUAGES

3 Describe in French the weather that goes with each picture.

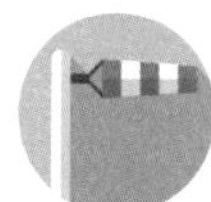

a. → ....

b. → ....

c. → ....

d. → ....

e. → ....

Prepositions of time
(Les prépositions de temps)

Talking about 'when'	
à [a]	*at*
après [apreh]	*after*
avant [avah^n]	*before*
dans [dah^n]	*in*
de... à... [duh a]	*from ... to ...*
depuis [duhpew-ee]	*for / since*
en [ah^n]	*in*
entre [ah^{n}tr]	*between*
jusqu'à [jzewska]	*until*
pendant [pah^{n}dah^n]	*for / during*
vers [vehr]	*at around*

4 Complete the sentences with the correct prepositions of time.

a. J'arrive à l'école .... 8 h.

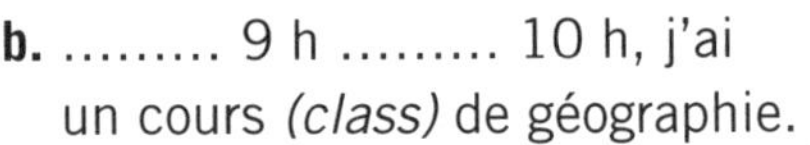
b. .... 9 h .... 10 h, j'ai un cours *(class)* de géographie.

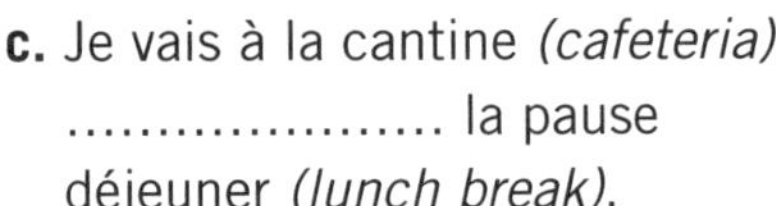
c. Je vais à la cantine *(cafeteria)* .... la pause déjeuner *(lunch break)*.

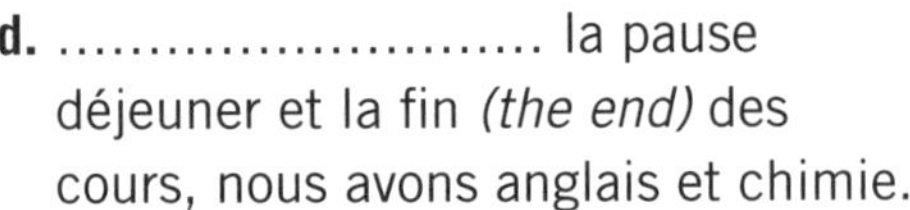
d. .... la pause déjeuner et la fin *(the end)* des cours, nous avons anglais et chimie.

e. J'ai des cours .... 16 h.

5 Translate these sentences into English.

a. Je me couche vers 22 h. ➜ ....

b. Je te téléphone dans 10 minutes. ➜ ....

c. Je rentre à la maison avant midi. ➜ ....

d. Je fais mes devoirs après le dîner. ➜ ....

e. Je suis à la piscine depuis ce matin. ➜ ....

The months *(Les mois)*

janvier [jzah^{n}vee-ay]	*January*
février [fayvree-ay]	*February*
mars [mars]	*March*
avril [avreel]	*April*
mai [meh]	*May*
juin [jzew-a^n]	*June*

juillet [jzew-ee-eh]	*July*
août [oot]	*August*
septembre [septah^{n}br]	*September*
octobre [oktobr]	*October*
novembre [novah^{n}br]	*November*
décembre [daysah^{n}br]	*December*

The months in French are all masculine nouns. They are often used with the preposition **en** *in*. Unlike in English, they are not capitalized: **en janvier** *in January*.

6 **Unscramble the letters of these months in French.**

a. tmeeepbsr = ...

b. rriéefv = ...

c. ultjiel = ...

d. inuj = ...

e. rdmecéeb = ...

f. rniejva = ...

Days of the week *(Les jours de la semaine)*

lundi [la^{n}dee]	*Monday*
mardi [mardee]	*Tuesday*
mercredi [mehrkruhdee]	*Wednesday*
jeudi [jzuhdee]	*Thursday*
vendredi [vah^{n}druhdee]	*Friday*
samedi [samdee]	*Saturday*
dimanche [deemah^{n}sh]	*Sunday*

All the days of the week are masculine. As with the months of the year, the days are not capitalized in French. They are not used with a preposition in most contexts (see the panel on the right).

Days of the week *(Les jours de la semaine)*

- In French, the preposition *on* is not used before the day of the week: **Je pars en vacances lundi.** *I am leaving on holiday (on) Monday.*
- To express something that happens regularly on a certain day of the week (e.g. *on Mondays*), the definite article **le** + the day (in the singular) is used: **Je vais à la piscine le lundi.** *I go to the swimming pool on Mondays.*
- To ask a date: **Quelle est la date aujourd'hui ?** *What's the date today?*
- The date is given with a cardinal number (but see below) + month: **Aujourd'hui, nous sommes le 25 octobre 2017.** *Today is* ('we are') *the 25th of* ('25') *October 2017.*
- For the first of the month, an ordinal number is used: **le 1er (le premier)** *the first*: **le 1er janvier**.

7 **Write out the dates following the example.**

E.g. 12/10/2008 → **Aujourd'hui, nous sommes le 12 octobre 2008.**

a. 02/02/2012 → ....

b. 05/09/2010 → ....

c. 29/04/2005 → ....

d. 01/08/2003 → ....

e. 15/06/2013 → ....

8 Translate these sentences into French.

a. I don't go to school on Saturdays. ➜ ....

b. I am going to the cinema on Sunday. ➜ ....

c. I have geography on Tuesdays. ➜ ....

d. I go to my grandparents on Wednesdays. ➜ ....

e. She is going to the dentist on Friday. ➜ ....

Adverbs of frequency *(Les adverbes de fréquence)*

Adverbs that express how often something is done usually come directly after the verb. To say that you never do something, the negative construction **ne... jamais...** is used: **Je <u>ne</u> vais <u>jamais</u> au cinéma.** *I never go to the cinema.* **Je <u>n</u>'ai <u>jamais</u> mangé de tomates.** *I have never eaten tomatoes.*

Adverbs of frequency *(Les adverbes de fréquence)*

Talking about 'how often'	
jamais [jzameh]	*never*
rarement [rarmah^n]	*rarely*
quelquefois [kehlkuhfwa] **parfois** [parfwa]	*sometimes*
de temps en temps [duh tah^n zah^n tah^n]	*from time to time*
généralement [jzaynayralmah^n]	*generally*
souvent [soovah^n]	*often*
toujours [toojzoor]	*always*

9 Underline the right adverb for each context.

a. Un coiffeur travaille **rarement / souvent** debout *(standing up)*.

b. Un chanteur travaille **quelquefois / souvent** le soir.

c. Un professeur travaille **rarement / généralement** après les cours *(lessons)*.

d. Un boulanger travaille **quelquefois / toujours** très tôt le matin.

e. Une infirmière travaille **quelquefois / généralement** de longues heures.

10 **Conjugate the verbs in the present tense using *ne... jamais...*.**

E.g. Elle (regarder) **ne regarde jamais** la télé.

a. Ils (téléphoner) .... à leurs cousins.

b. Nous (écouter) .... de musique classique.

c. Vous (finir) .... vos pâtes !

d. Tu (entendre) .... les questions du professeur.

e. Je (perdre) .... mes clés.

Periods of time *(Les durées)*

The masculine terms **l'an** *the year*, **le jour** *the day*, **le matin** *the morning* and **le soir** *the evening* are used when referring to a single point in time. The corresponding feminine terms **l'année, la journée, la matinée** and **la soirée** refer to a duration or length of time.

Time words *(Les indicateurs temporels)*

Talking about 'when' and 'how long'	
un an [ahⁿ] **/ une année** [anay]	*a year*
aujourd'hui [ohjzoordew-ee]	*today*
demain [duhmaⁿ]	*tomorrow*
dernier [dehrnee-ay] **/ dernière** [dehrnee-ehr]	*last*
hier [ee-ehr]	*yesterday*
un jour [jzoor] **/ une journée** [jzoornay]	*a day*
maintenant [maⁿtuhnahⁿ]	*now*
un matin [mataⁿ] **/ une matinée** [mateenay]	*a morning*
midi [meedee]	*noon*
un mois [mwa]	*a month*
prochain [proshaⁿ] **/ prochaine** [proshehn]	*next*
une semaine [suhmehn]	*a week*
un soir [swar] **/ une soirée** [swaray]	*an evening*

11 **Complete the sentences with the time words.**

hier - prochaine - aujourd'hui - matin - maintenant - soir

a. Nous allons au restaurant ce .... à 19 h.

b. ...., je ne vais pas à l'école : c'est dimanche !

c. Mets tes chaussures et ton manteau ! Nous partons .... !

d. Nous partons en vacances la semaine ....

e. Ils sont allés au musée ....

f. Il a un cours de biologie le lundi .... de 9 h à 10 h.

Génial ! You've completed Lesson 13! It's time to count up the icons for the exercises and record your results here and in the table on page 127.

14

Talking about location

(prepositions and adverbs of place)

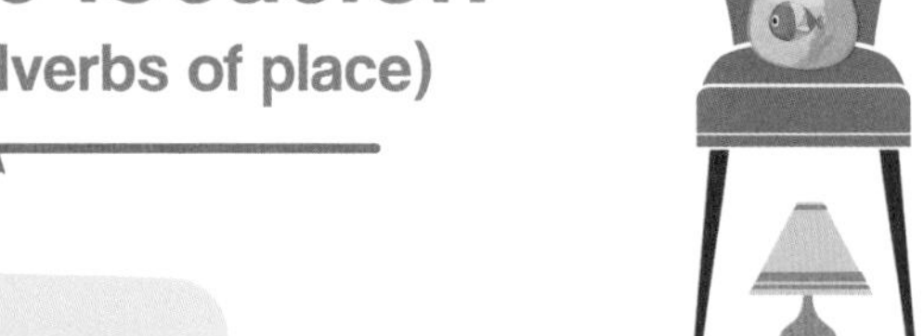

Prepositions and adverbs of place *(Les prépositions et les adverbes de lieu)*

The word preposition literally means 'placed in front of'. A preposition (e.g. **à** *at*, **dans** *in*, **sur** *on*) is usually used in front of a noun or a pronoun and shows the relationship of the noun/pronoun to other words in the sentence. For example, to describe where someone/something is: **Il est <u>derrière</u> la maison.** *He is <u>behind</u> the house.*

- Prepositional phrases include **à côté de** *next to*, **en dessous de** *underneath.*
- An adverb is a word or a phrase that modifies an adjective, verb or other adverb to express manner, place, time or degree: **Elle mange <u>vite</u>.** *She eats <u>quickly</u>.*
- Note that some prepositions can be used as adverbs: **Je l'ai rangé <u>dessous</u>.** *I put it <u>underneath</u>.*

Prepositions and adverbs of place ***(Les prépositions et les adverbes de lieu)***

Prepositions	Adverbs	
dans [dah^n], **en** [ah^n]	**dedans** [duhdah^n]	*in, within, into, inside*
sur [sewr], **au-dessus de*** [oh duhsew duh]	**dessus, au-dessus**	*on, on top of, over, above*
sous [soo], **en dessous de*** [ah^n duhsoo duh]	**dessous, en dessous**	*under, underneath, below*
à côté de* [a kohtay duh]	**à côté**	*next to, beside, alongside*
devant [duhvah^n]	**devant**	*in front of*
derrière [dehree-ehr]	**derrière, à l'arrière**	*behind*
entre [ah^{n}tr]	-	*between*
parmi [parmee]	-	*among*
contre [koh^{n}tr]	**contre**	*against*

Prepositions	Adverbs	
près de* [preh duh]	**(tout** [too]**) près**	*near*
loin de* [lwa^n duh]	**loin**	*far, a long way from*
en face de* [ah^n fas duh]	**en face**	*opposite*
au milieu de* [oh meelee-uh duh]	**au milieu**	*in the middle (of)*
à droite de* [a drwat duh]	**à droite**	*to the right (of)*
à gauche de* [a gohsh duh]	**à gauche**	*to the left (of)*
en bas de* [ah^n ba duh]	**en bas**	*down below, downstairs*
en haut de* [ah^n oh duh]	**en haut**	*up above, upstairs*
vers [vehr]	-	*towards*

* If the word after these expressions is masculine, **du** is used (never **de le**).

Complete the sentences using these words expressing location.

sous - dans - sur - entre - devant - loin de

a. Les toilettes sont .... la chambre et la cuisine.

b. Ton manteau est .... le garage.

c. Le cinéma est très .... notre maison ! Nous devons y aller en voiture *(car)*.

d. La pizza est .... la table de la cuisine.

e. Le chien se cache *(is hiding)* .... le lit de mes parents.

f. Claire est dans le canapé, ... la télévision.

2 Translate the sentences above into English.

a. ....

b. ....

c. ....

d. ....

e. ....

f. ....

3 Use the pictures to fill in the missing prepositions.

a. Le chat est .... le carton.

b. Le chat est .... le carton.

c. Le chat est .... le carton.

d. Le chat est .... le carton.

e. Le chat est .... le carton.

f. Le chat est .... deux cartons.

g. Le chat est .... du carton.

h. Le chat est .... du carton.

4 Underline the correct preposition or adverb in each context.

a. – Où est ma chemise ? – Elle est **dans / dedans** le sac.

b. Regarde ! Sophie est **côté / à côté** de Florian !

c. – Où est la voiture ? – Elle est là : regarde, **à gauche / à gauche de**.

d. – Les clés sont-elles dans le sac ? – Non, elles sont **en dessous / en dessous de**.

e. La pharmacie est **en face / en face de** la boulangerie.

f. Le parc est **au milieu / au milieu de** la ville.

Prepositions with geographical names (*Les prépositions avec noms géographiques*)

Like all French nouns, the names of cities, countries, continents and other geographical locations have a gender. The gender determines which preposition to use with the name. Generally, place names that end in **-e** are feminine (so take **en**), while others are masculine (so take **au**, unless they start with a vowel). But there are exceptions – you'll just have to learn these!

Cities (and certain islands)	**à**	*to, in*	**Paris** **Barcelone** **Londres**
Masculine countries starting with a consonant	**au**		**Japon** **Portugal**
Feminine countries, continents, and masculine countries starting with a vowel	**en**		**Europe** **Asie** **Suède** **Afrique**
Plural countries	**aux**		**États-Unis**

5 Complete these sentences using à, au, en or aux.

a. Je vais .... Milan la semaine prochaine *(next week)*.

b. Corentin est .... Australie en ce moment *(at the moment)*.

c. Le cousin d'Edwige habite .... Canada.

d. Julien est parti .... États-Unis ce matin *(this morning)*.

e. Sophie rêve d'aller *(dreams of going)* .... Chine.

f. La tour Eiffel se situe .... Paris.

6 Create complete sentences from the elements given, as shown in the example.

E.g. Line / Asker / Norvège → **Line habite à Asker, en Norvège.**

a. Aiko / Nagoya / Japon ....

b. Elvis / Tupelo / États-Unis ....

c. Myriam / Boismorand / France ....

d. Marco / Cascais / Portugal ....

e. Chloé / Bruges / Belgique ....

f. Louis / Québec / Canada ....

à and *chez*

- The preposition **chez** *at, to* is used for locations related to a particular person: **Il est chez Mariette.** *He is at Mariette's.* **Il va chez Mariette.** *He is going to Mariette's.*
- Use **à** *at, to* to refer more generally to a place. **Je vais à l'école.** *I'm going to school.*

à + place (**à** + **le** = **au**, **à** + **les** = **aux**)	**à l'école** **à la piscine** **au restaurant** **aux urgences** *(A&E, ER)*
chez + person	**chez Christophe** **chez mes parents** **chez le dentiste**

Places in the city *(Lieux dans la ville)*

l'aéroport [a-ayropor]	*airport*
la banque [bah^{n}k]	*bank*
la bibliothèque [beebleeyotehk]	*library*
la boulangerie [boolah^{n}jzree]	*bakery*
le cinéma [seenayma]	*cinema*
le dentiste [dah^{n}teest]	*dentist*
l'église [aygleez]	*church*
la gare [gar]	*train station*
l'hôpital [opeetal]	*hospital*
l'hôtel [ohtehl]	*hotel*
la librairie [leebrehree]	*bookshop*
le magasin [magaza^n]	*shop / store*

le marché [marshay]	*market*
le médecin [mehdsa^n]/ **le docteur** [doktuhr]	*the doctor's*
le musée [mewzay]	*museum*
la pâtisserie [pateesree]	*cake shop*
la pharmacie [farmasee]	*pharmacy / chemist's*
la piscine [peeseen]	*swimming pool*
la place [plas]	*square*
la poste [post]	*post office*
le théâtre [tay-atr]	*theater*
les urgences [ewrjzah^{n}s]	*emergency service*

7 Translate these sentences into English.

a. Corinne est à la maison. ....

b. Carlos va chez Paul samedi. ....

c. Oh, non ! Mon sac est chez ta grand-mère ! ....
....

d. Les enfants jouent au parc. ....

e. Éloïse est à l'hôpital ! ....

8 Circle the right preposition in each case.

a. Je suis arrivé **à l' / à la / au / chez** école à 9 h.

b. Tu vas **à l' / à la / au / chez** piscine demain *(tomorrow)* ?

c. Éric est allé **à l' / à la / au / chez** Caroline dimanche.

d. Luc est arrivé **à l' / à la / au / chez** musée à 17 h.

e. Maman a rendez-vous *(an appointment)* **à l' / à la / au / chez** le docteur mardi.

f. Charles va **à l' / à la / au / chez** mer *(sea*, f.*)* en vacances.

9 Unscramble the letters of each French place, and then write it with the correct definite article.

E.g. oepst → **poste** → **la poste**

a. mhaaeiprc → .... → ....

b. reugesnc → .... → ....

c. sneidtte → .... → ....

d. éeislg → .... → ....

e. ièbbtiuholeq → .... → ....

f. plaôhit → .... → ....

'To' and 'from' *(à et de)*

- To indicate that you are going somewhere (or are already there), **à** is used: **Je vais à la gare.** *I'm going to the train station.* **Je suis à Madrid.** *I'm in Madrid.*
- To indicate that you are coming (or originate) from somewhere, **de** is used: **Je viens de la pharmacie.** *I'm coming from the pharmacy.* **Je suis de Paris.** *I'm from Paris.*

10 Match up the elements to form sentences. 

1) Je vais
2) JE VIENS

a) à la bibliothèque.
b) aux urgences.
c) du cinema.
d) de la poste.
e) au théâtre.
f) du musée.
g) de Sydney.
h) à la gare.

Bravo! You've completed Lesson 14! It's time to count up the icons for the exercises and record your results here and in the table on page 127.

15 Making commands & requests

The imperative *(L'impératif)*

- The imperative is the verb form used to give orders or make requests.
- Since commands are addressed to another person, in French, there are two conjugations that correspond to the different forms of *you*: **tu** (informal singular) and **vous** (plural as well as formal singular and plural). There is also a **nous** conjugation, which translates to the suggestion *Let's ...* .
- The imperative has the same conjugation as the present tense, but as in English, the verb is used without the subject pronoun (**tu**, **nous**, **vous**).

tu imperative	**Prends le livre !**	*Take the book!* (informal sing.)
nous imperative	**Prenons le livre !**	*Let's take the book!*
vous imperative	**Prenez le livre !**	*Take the book!* (plural / formal sing.)

- However, for verbs ending in **-er**, the final **-s** is dropped in the second-person singular (**tu** imperative): **Chante !** *Sing!* → **Ne chante pas !** *Don't sing!* (informal)
- Some common verbs are irregular in the imperative:

	avoir *to have*	**être** *to be*	**savoir** *to know*	**vouloir*** *to want*
tu imperative	**aie**	**sois**	**sache**	**veuille**
nous imperative	**ayons**	**soyons**	**sachons**	**veuillons**
vous imperative	**ayez**	**soyez**	**sachez**	**veuillez**

*The imperative of **vouloir** is used to make polite, formal requests, so **veuillez** is the only form used today. It basically translates to *please*: **Veuillez patienter.** *Please wait.*

1 **Circle the correct form of the imperative in these sentences.** 

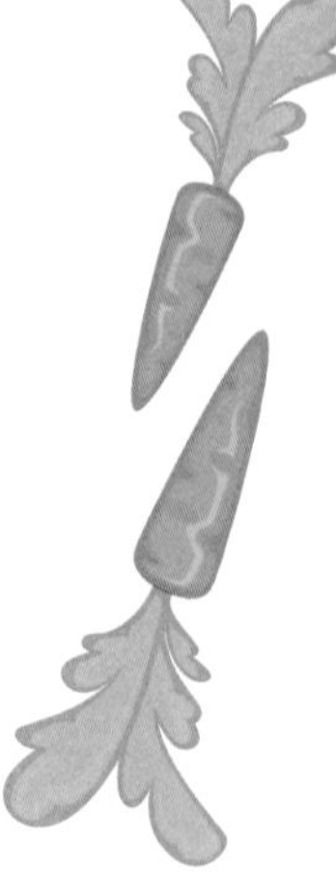

a. (tu) **Mange / Mangeons / Mangez** tes carottes !

b. (vous) **Aie / Ayons / Ayez** du respect pour vos parents !

c. (nous) **Finis / Finissons / Finissez** l'exercice de la page 32.

d. (vous) **Obéis / Obéissons / Obéissez** à vos parents !

e. (tu) **Lave / Lavons / Lavez** ton assiette *(your plate)*, s'il te plaît *(please)*.

f. (nous) **Vends / Vendons / Vendez** nos vieux livres.

2 Conjugate these verbs in the correct person of the imperative.

E.g. (regarder/tu) les beaux oiseaux ! → **Regarde les beaux oiseaux !**

a. (arrêter/tu) .... de parler avec Julien !

b. (prendre/vous) .... les valises, s'il vous plaît.

c. (écouter/tu) .... le professeur !

d. (être/nous) .... généreux !

e. (vouloir/vous) .... entrer dans l'église silencieusement *(quietly)*.

f. (partir/tu) .... à huit heures.

3 Translate these commands into French.

a. Eat (**vous**) your bread! ....

b. Get out (**tu**) of the bathroom! ....

c. Let's go to the library! ....

d. Let's watch a movie! ....

e. Read (**vous**) the exercise on p.16. ....

f. Take (**tu**) a biscuit! ....

The negative imperative *(L'impératif négatif)*

A negative imperative is a prohibition, i.e. telling someone not to do something. This is formed simply by placing **ne... pas...** around the imperative verb: **Ne mange pas ces champignons !** *Don't eat those mushrooms!*

4 Put the words in the right order to form commands.

a. ne / à / Sophie / téléphone / pas ....

b. pas / votre / ne / adresse / donnez ....

c. les / finissez / pas / ne / oranges ....

d. tes / pas / perds / ne / clés *(keys)* ....

e. ne / maison / aujourd'hui / choisissons / pas / une ....

....

5 Translate the sentences from the previous exercise into English.

a. ....

b. ....

c. ....

d. ....

e. ....

f. ....

The imperative with object pronouns *(L'impératif avec les pronoms objets)*

In affirmative commands, an object pronoun comes after the verb and is joined to it with a hyphen: **Range-les** ! *Put them away!* **Vendez-la** ! *Sell it!*

6 Circle the correct object pronoun.

E.g. les verres → Remplissez-le / la / (les) !

a. l'assiette *(the plate)* → Lave-**le** / **la** / **les** !

b. la maison → Bâtis-**le** / **la** / **les** !

c. l'exercice → Finissez-**le** / **la** / **les** !

d. les problèmes → Explique-**le** / **la** / **les** !

e. le train → Prends-**le** / **la** / **les** !

7 Write the commands using an imperative and an object pronoun.

E.g. Tu vois le livre ? (lire) → **Lis-le** !

a. Vous voyez les enfants ? (appeler) .... !

b. Tu vois les bonbons ? (donner) .... !

c. Vous voyez la chaise ? (vendre) .... !

d. Tu vois la salade ? (prendre) .... !

e. Vous voyez la bouteille *(bottle)* ? (remplir) .... !

f. Tu vois l'exercice p. 4 ? (finir) .... !

The imperative of reflexive verbs
(L'impératif des verbes pronominaux)

The imperative of reflexive verbs (e.g. **se lever** *to get up*) is formed in the same way as a command with an object pronoun. However, the reflexive pronouns become emphatic pronouns: **toi**, **nous**, **vous**.

Lève-toi ! *Get up!* **Réveillons-nous !** *Let's wake up!* **Habillez-vous !** *Get dressed!*

8 **Turn the statements into commands.**

E.g. Tu t'amuses. → **Amuse-toi** !

a. Vous vous douchez. → .... !

b. Nous nous levons. → .... !

c. Tu te couches. → .... !

d. Tu te promènes. → .... !

e. Vous vous réveillez. → .... !

Finding your way around
(Trouver son chemin)

- A polite way to ask for directions is: **Excusez-moi, où est ... / où se trouve ... ?** *Excuse me, where is ... ? / where is ... located?*
- When giving directions, the imperative is usually used: **Tourne(z) à gauche.** *Turn left.*

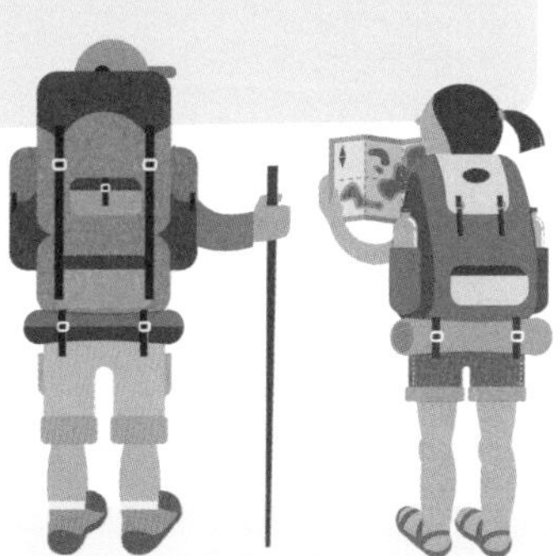

Asking and giving directions
(Demander et donner des directions)

à droite [a drwat]	*on/to the right*
à gauche [a gohsh]	*on/to the left*
au coin de la rue [oh kwa^n duh la rew]	*on/at the corner*
après [apreh]	*after*
avant [avah^n]	*before*
continuer [koh^{n}teenew-ay]	*to carry on*
derrière [dehree-ehr]	*behind*
devant [duhvah^n]	*in front of*
en face de [ah^n fas duh]	*opposite*
prendre [prah^{n}dr]	*to take*
tourner [toornay]	*to turn*
tout droit [too drwa]	*straight ahead*
traverser [travehrsay]	*to cross*

9 Match up the French terms with their English equivalents.

droite	*to turn*
gauche	*in front of*
devant	*right*
derrière	*to carry on*
tourner	*behind*
traverser	*left*
continuer	*to cross*

10 Translate these sentences into French.

a. Turn right after the church. (**vous**) → ....

b. Carry on straight ahead. (**tu**) → ....

c. The pharmacy is behind the museum. → ....

d. The station is across from the swimming pool. → ....

....

e. Take the first street (**rue**) on the left. (**vous**) → ....

....

Nice work! You've completed Lesson 15! It's time to count up the icons for the exercises and record your results here and in the table on page 127.

16
The future

The future tense *(Le futur)*

- In French as in English, the future tense is used to talk about an action or a state that will occur in the future. The difference in French is that the future tense conjugates as a single word rather than using an auxiliary verb (e.g. *will*).
- For regular verbs, the future is easy to conjugate: all three verb groups (**-er**, **-ir** and **-re**) take the same endings, which are simply added to the infinitive. However, the **-re** verbs drop the final **-e** of the infinitive before adding the conjugation endings.

	aimer	finir	vendre
je/j'	aimerai	finirai	vendrai
tu	aimeras	finiras	vendras
il/elle	aimera	finira	vendra
nous	aimerons	finirons	vendrons
vous	aimerez	finirez	vendrez
ils/elles	aimeront	finiront	vendront

Note: the endings for the **je**, **tu**, **il/elle** and **ils/elles** forms are the same as the present tense of **avoir**. The **nous** ending is **-ons**, and the **vous** ending is **-ez**.

1 **Complete the sentences using the appropriate verb in the future from the suitcase.**

a. Nous .... le train samedi à 14 h.

b. Elles .... en voiture dimanche matin.

c. J' .... un sandwich à la gare.

d. Jean .... le chemin *(way)* de l'hôtel.

e. Tu .... un taxi pour aller au restaurant.

f. Vous .... la carte *(map)* pour trouver votre chemin.

2 Conjugate the following verbs in the correct person of the future tense.

a. Alice (regarder) .... la télévision avec Marco.

b. Anne et Alex (rendre) *(give back)* .... la voiture à leurs parents.

c. Vous (bâtir) .... une nouvelle maison en centre-ville.

d. Nous (descendre) .... du bus car *(because)* nous sommes en retard.

e. Tu (danser) .... toute la nuit !

f. Je (choisir) .... un nouveau livre.

Irregular verbs in the future tense *(Verbes irréguliers au futur)*

- As in the present tense, verbs ending in **e** + consonant + **er** (such as **acheter** and **appeler**) take an accent (**è**) in the future or sometimes double the consonant: **j'achèterai** *I will buy*, **tu appelleras** *you will call*.

Some irregular verbs in the future ***(Quelques verbes irréguliers au futur)***

Some verbs do not use the infinitive as the stem in the future. Here are some of these:

- **aller** *to go*: **j'irai, tu iras, il/elle ira, nous irons, vous irez, ils/elles iront**
- **avoir** *to have*: **j'aurai, tu auras, il/elle aura, nous aurons, vous aurez, ils/elles auront**
- **courir** *to run*: **je courrai, tu courras, il/elle courra, nous courrons, vous courrez, ils/elles courront**
- **devoir** *to have to, must*: **je devrai, tu devras, il/elle devra, nous devrons, vous devrez, ils/elles devront**
- **envoyer** *to send*: **j'enverrai, tu enverras, il/elle enverra, nous enverrons, vous enverrez, ils/elles enverront**
- **être** *to be*: **je serai, tu seras, il/elle sera, nous serons, vous serez, ils/elles seront**
- **faire** *to do*: **je ferai, tu feras, il/elle fera, nous ferons, vous ferez, ils/elles feront**
- **mourir** *to die*: **je mourrai, tu mourras, il/elle mourra, nous mourrons, vous mourrez, ils/elles mourront**
- **pouvoir** *to be able to, can*: **je pourrai, tu pourras, il/elle pourra, nous pourrons, vous pourrez, ils/elles pourront**
- **savoir** *to know*: **je saurai, tu sauras, il/elle saura, nous saurons, vous saurez, ils/elles sauront**
- **tenir** *to hold*: **je tiendrai, tu tiendras, il/elle tiendra, nous tiendrons, vous tiendrez, ils/elles tiendront**
- **venir** *to come*: **je viendrai, tu viendras, il/elle viendra, nous viendrons, vous viendrez, ils/elles viendront**
- **voir** *to see*: **je verrai, tu verras, il/elle verra, nous verrons, vous verrez, ils/elles verront**
- **vouloir** *to want*: **je voudrai, tu voudras, il/elle voudra, nous voudrons, vous voudrez, ils/elles voudront**

 **Underline the 10 verbs in the future tense.** 

Charlotte est contente : son frère, Éric, arrivera demain de Paris et passera une semaine avec elle. Ils iront au musée des sciences puis mangeront au restaurant. Éric partira ensuite pendant deux jours et verra son ami Philippe à Tours : « Tu viendras avec moi ? » demandera Éric à Charlotte. « Oui, peut-être ! J'irai voir mon amie Sophie ! » répondra Charlotte.

 **Circle the correct form of these irregular verbs.** 

a. Elle **saurai / sauras / saura** si elle part à Paris samedi.

b. Viendrons / Viendra / Viendras-tu avec ta sœur au cinéma ?

c. Nous **serez / sera / serons** très heureux de venir vous voir.

d. Tu ne **devrai / devras / devrez** pas te lever à 8 h.

e. Ferai / Ferez / Feront-vous un gâteau pour la fête *(party)* de Mélanie ?

f. Caroline et Stéphanie **verrons / verront / veront** le nouveau film de Jean Dujardin vendredi prochain.

5 Conjugate the verbs in the future tense to complete the sentences.

a. Nous (venir) .... vous voir dimanche à midi.

b. Je ne (voir) .... pas Colette demain soir.

c. Vous (pouvoir) .... manger des bonbons après le dîner.

d. Maéva (faire) .... ses devoirs *(homework)* ce week-end.

e. Paula et Aymeric (devoir) .... aider leurs parents dans le jardin.

f. Tu (courir) .... pour aller à l'école !

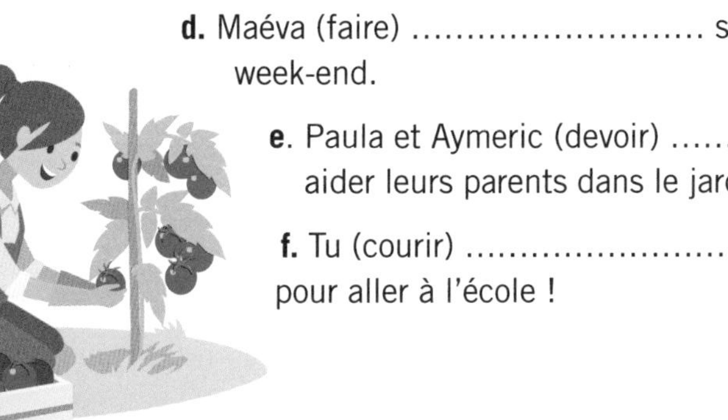

The near future *(Le futur proche)*

- As in English, it is very common in spoken French to talk about something that is fairly certain to happen in the near future, using the verb **aller** *to go* conjugated in the present tense + infinitive: **Je vais partir en vacances demain.** *I'm going to leave on holiday tomorrow.* **Il va manger au restaurant ce soir.** *He's going to eat at a restaurant tonight.*
- It's also possible to simply use the present tense to express something that will take place shortly: **Demain, je mange au restaurant.** *I'm eating at a restaurant tomorrow.*

6 **Conjugate the verb *aller* in the present tense.**

je .... il/elle .... vous ....

tu .... nous .... ils/elles ....

7 **Use the near future (with aller) to complete these sentences.**

E.g. Nous (aider) **allons aider** Karine à faire ses devoirs dimanche.

a. Vite *(Quick)*! Vous **(rater)** *(miss)* .... le bus !

b. Nous **(voir)** .... Lucie à l'hôpital jeudi prochain.

c. Corentin **(écouter)** .... son nouveau CD ce soir.

d. Clarice et Lison **(manger)** .... tous les bonbons !

e. Je **(téléphoner)** .... à ton professeur demain.

f. Ils **(choisir)** .... leurs matières *(subjects)* l'année prochaine.

The near future in the negative (*La négation au futur proche*)

- The **ne... pas** is placed around the conjugated auxiliary verb **aller**:
Elle <u>ne</u> va <u>pas</u> aller au cinéma ce soir. *She's not going to the cinema tonight.*
Il <u>ne</u> va <u>pas</u> se lever à 8 heures demain matin. *He's not going to wake up at 8:00 tomorrow morning.*

8 Rewrite these sentences in the negative.

a. J'irai au Portugal l'année prochaine. ➜ ....

....

b. Nous allons voir l'Arc de Triomphe à Paris. ➜ ....

....

c. Ils vont manger tous les haricots verts *(green beans)* et le brocoli. ➜ ....

....

d. Vous visiterez le Canada en train. ➜ ....

....

e. Audrey va prendre le bus pour aller à Tours. ➜ ....

....

9 Translate these sentences into French.

a. I will not watch TV. ➜ ....

b. They are going to wait for (**attendre**) the bus. ➜ ....

....

c. Sonia is not going to lose (**perdre**) her handbag (**sac à main**). ➜ ....

....

d. The train will not leave at 10 a.m. ➜ ....

....

e. Philippe is going to answer the questions. ➜ ....

....

Fill in the crossword with these verb forms in French.

a. you (sing.) will read – he/she/it will do

c. they will want

e. you (sing.) will love

h. I will be

i. he/she will paint

j. I will love

l. you (pl.) will ask

1. you (sing.) will get up (**tu te** ______________)

3. you (pl.) will come

5. I will know

7. he/she/it will fill

8. I have

9. we will finish

11. you (pl.) will hope

13. I will believe

	1	2	3	4	5	6	7	8	9	10	11	12	13
a	___	___	___	___	___				___	___	___	___	
b	___				___				___				___
c	___		___	___	___	___	___	___	___	___			___
d	___		___		___		___		___		___		___
e	___		___		___	___	___	___	___	___	___		___
f	___		___		___		___		___		___		___
g	___		___				___		___		___		___
h			___				___		___	___	___	___	___
i		___	___	___	___	___	___	___			___		
j			___				___	___	___	___	___	___	___
k											___		
l		___	___	___	___	___	___	___	___	___	___		

Chapeau! You've reached the end of Lesson 16! It's time to count up the icons for the exercises and record your result here and on page 127.

17 Adverbs

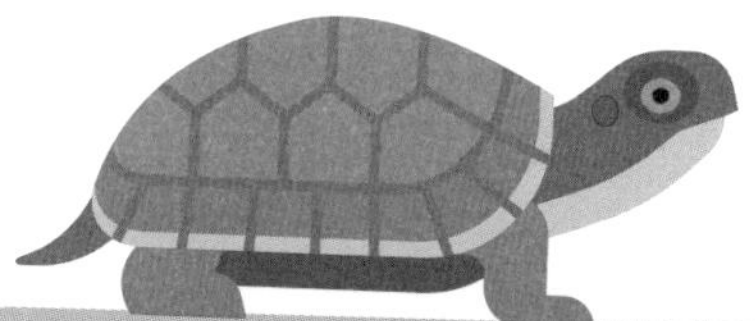

The formation of adverbs *(La formation des adverbes)*

- An adverb is a word that modifies a verb, an adjective or another adverb to provide more information about it.
- In English, many adverbs are formed by adding *-ly* to an adjective. In French, a similar process is followed, using the suffix **-ment**. For these adverbs (many of which are adverbs of manner), the suffix is added to the masculine form of the adjective if it ends in a vowel (**rapide** *quick* → **rapidement** *quickly*, **absolu** *absolute* → **absolument** *absolutely*, **vrai** *true* → **vraiment** *truly*) or to the feminine form of the adjective if it ends in a consonant (**lent** *slow* → **lente** → **lentement** *slowly*).
- There are, however, some exceptions to this rule: **bref** *brief* → **brièvement** *briefly*, **gentil** *nice* → **gentiment** *nicely*.
- Adjectives ending in **-ant** change to **-amment** and in **-ent** to **-emment**: **courant** *common* → **couramment** *commonly*, **patient** *patient* → **patiemment** *patiently*.
- A few other adverbs end in **-ément**, such as **précisément** *exactly* and **énormément** *enormously*.

1 Turn the following adjectives into adverbs.

a. joli → ....

b. triste → ....

c. grand → ....

d. léger → ....

e. joyeux → ....

f. gentil → ....

g. suffisant *(sufficient)* → ....

Adverbs of manner *(Les adverbes de manière)*

- An adverb of manner expresses how something is done. In French, these often end in **-ment** (e.g. **rapidement** *quickly*, **lentement** *slowly*, **sérieusement** *seriously*).
- Here are a few common adverbs of manner that don't end in **-ment** with their corresponding adjectives.

Adjectives		Adverbs	
bon [boh^{n}]	*good*	**bien** [bee-a^{n}]	*well*
mauvais [moveh]	*bad*	**mal** [mal]	*badly*
meilleur [meh-yuhr]	*better*	**mieux** [mee-uh]	*better*

2 Complete the sentences with the appropriate adjective or adverb below. Note whether it is an adjective (ADJ) or an adverb (ADV).

rapidement - mauvais - gentiment - bien - jolie - bon - meilleur

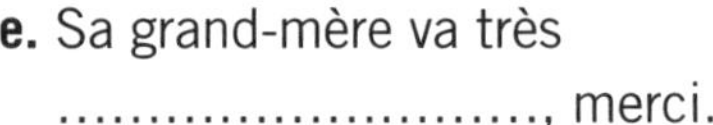

a. C'est le .... gâteau de la pâtisserie.

b. Sa mère m'a parlé ....

c. Ce dessert était très ....

d. Elle entre dans la banque .... car son bus arrive dans cinq minutes.

e. Sa grand-mère va très ...., merci.

f. Demain, il fera .... Il y aura beaucoup de nuages.

g. Carla est vraiment .... aujourd'hui avec sa robe rouge !

Adverbs of frequency *(Les adverbes de fréquence)*

These are usually placed after the verb.

- -	**jamais**	*never*
-	**rarement**	*rarely*
+	**quelquefois** **parfois** **de temps en temps**	*sometimes* *at times* *occasionally*
+ +	**souvent** **généralement**	*often* *generally*
+ + +	**toujours** **tout le temps**	*always* *all the time*

3 Circle the appropriate adverb of frequency in each context.

a. Un coiffeur parle **rarement / généralement** avec ses clients *(customers).*

b. Une boulangère vend **rarement / toujours** du pain.

c. Un fermier travaille **parfois / toujours** avec un ordinateur *(computer).*

d. Une musicienne travaille **rarement / généralement** dans un bureau.

e. Un boucher vend **quelquefois / toujours** de la viande.

4 Translate these sentences into French.

a. I often go to the cinema. ➜ ....

b. My sister eats chocolate all the time. ➜ ....

....

c. They never read. ➜ ....

d. Henry sometimes gets up at 7 a.m. ➜ ....

....

e. The teacher never says hello. ➜ ....

Adverbs of time *(Les adverbes de temps)*

Adverbs of time answer the question **Quand ?** *When?* A reference to a specific point in time (e.g. **aujourd'hui**) can be placed at the beginning or the end of a sentence.

après [apreh]	*after*
après-demain [apreh duhma^n]	*the day after tomorrow*
aujourd'hui [ohjzoordew-ee]	*today*
autrefois [ohtruhfwa]	*in the past*
avant [avah^n]	*before*
avant-hier [avah^n tee-ehr]	*the day before yesterday*
bientôt [bee-a^{n}toh]	*soon*
déjà [dayjza]	*already*
demain [duhma^n]	*tomorrow*
depuis [duhpew-ee]	*since*
ensuite [ah^{n}sew-eet]	*next*

hier [ee-ehr]	*yesterday*
il y a [eel ee ya]	*ago*
jamais [jzameh]	*never*
maintenant [ma^{n}tuhnah^n]	*now*
parfois [parfwa]	*sometimes*
puis [pew-ee]	*then*
rarement [rarmah^n]	*rarely*
souvent [soovah^n]	*often*
tard [tar]	*late*
tôt [toh]	*early*
toujours [toojzoor]	*always, still*
tout de suite [too duh sew-eet]	*immediately*

5 **Complete the sentences using the appropriate adverb below.**

DEMAIN - BIENTÔT - TARD - TÔT - SOUVENT - HIER - JAMAIS

a. Je ne vais .... au musée : c'est trop ennuyeux *(too boring)* !

b. Rachel ira chez ses grands-parents ....

c. Vous devez vous lever .... : le train part à 6 h !

d. Nous allons .... au cinéma car nous adorons voir les nouveaux films.

e. Tu ne peux pas rentrer après minuit : c'est trop .... !

f. ...., nous sommes allés chez le dentiste : c'était horrible !

g. Dépêchez-vous *(Hurry up)* ! Le bus va .... partir !

6 **Translate the sentences above into English.**

a. ....

b. ....

c. ....

d. ....

e. ....

f. ....

g. ....

Adverbs of place *(Les adverbes de lieu)*

Adverbs of place answer the question **Où ?** *Where?* They can be placed before or after the verb, but usually come after it.

à droite [a drwat]	*to the right*
à gauche [a gohsh]	*to the left*
à l'intérieur de [a la^{n}tehree-uhr duh]	*inside*
autour [ohtoor]	*around*
dehors [duh-or]	*outside*
devant [duhvah^n]	*in front of*
en bas [ah^n ba]	*downstairs*
en haut [ah^n oh]	*upstairs*

ici [eesee]	*here*
là [la]	*there*
là-bas [la ba]	*over there*
près [preh]	*near*
loin [lwa^n]	*far*
nulle part [newl par]	*nowhere*
partout [partoo]	*everywhere*
quelque part [kelkuh par]	*somewhere*

7 Complete the sentences using the appropriate adverb(s) below. 

EN HAUT - DEHORS - EN BAS - PARTOUT - LÀ-BAS - LOIN - NULLE PART

a. Je n'ai pas trouvé *(found)* mes clés. J'ai cherché ....
mais je ne les ai trouvées ....

b. « Où est maman ? – Elle est ...., regarde, à côté de la voiture sur le parking *(car park)* ! »

c. « Où est la valise *(suitcase)* ? – Elle est ...., à la cave. »

d. « Et les manteaux ? Où sont-ils ? – Ils sont ...., au grenier *(attic)*. »

e. « Peut-on aller à l'école à pied *(on foot)* ?
– Oh, non, c'est trop .... Nous irons à l'école en voiture ! »

f. « As-tu vu Rex ? – Oui, il est ...., dans le jardin. »

Adverbs of quantity *(Les adverbes de quantité)*

When used before a noun, these adverbs are followed by **de**.

Talking about 'how much' or 'how many'	
assez (de) [asay duh]	*enough*
beaucoup (de) [bohkoo duh]	*a lot*
peu (de) [puh duh]	*little, few*
plus (de) [plews duh]	*more*
trop (de) [troh duh]	*too much, too many*
un peu (de) [a^n puh duh]	*a little*

8 Complete the sentences using the appropriate adverb below.

Voulez-vous encore du café, madame ?

– Non merci, j'en ai **(a)** ....

– Et désirez-vous **(b)** .... sucre *(sugar)* ?

– Oh là là ! Non, il y en a déjà **(c)** .... !

– Du lait, peut-être *(perhaps)* ? En *(Of it)* voulez-vous **(d)** .... ?

– Oh non ! **(e)** ...., s'il vous plaît !!! J'adore le lait !

Interrogative adverbs (Les adverbes interrogatifs)

These are used to ask questions. (See pages 59–61 for more on asking questions and question words.) When used before a noun, **combien** is followed by **de**.

Combien (de) ? [kohⁿbee-aⁿ]	*How much/many?*
Comment ? [komahⁿ]	*How?* (sometimes *What?*)
Où ? [oo]	*Where?*
Pourquoi ? [poorkwa]	*Why?*
Quand ? [kahⁿ]	*When?*
Quel ? [kehl]	*What? Which?*
Qui ? [kee]	*Who?*

9 Complete the questions with the appropriate question word above.

a. « .... venez-vous à Paris ? – Nous venons vous voir en septembre. »

b. « .... es-tu triste ? – J'ai perdu mon chat ! »

c. « .... est ce garçon avec ta sœur ? – C'est Marc, son ami. »

d. « .... vas-tu aujourd'hui ? – Je vais bien.»

e. « .... est papa ? – Il est dans le garage. »

f. « .... de sucres veux-tu dans ton café ? – Deux, s'il te plaît. »

The position of adverbs *(La place des adverbes)*

- When an adverb qualifies the meaning of an adjective, the adverb comes before it: **Elle est vraiment jolie.** *She is really pretty.*
- An adverb that qualifies the meaning of a verb usually comes after it: **Julie est rentrée rapidement.** *Julie came back quickly.*
- With compound verbs (verbs made up of more than one word), long adverbs come after the past participle: **Carlos a mangé lentement.** *Carlos ate slowly.* (Exceptions include **certainement** *certainly*, **complètement** *completely*, **probablement** *probably*: **Il est probablement parti.** *He has probably left.*)
- Short adverbs, e.g. **bien** *well*, **souvent** *often*, **mal** *badly*, **beaucoup** *a lot*, come before the past participle: **J'ai bien mangé.** *I ate well.*
- In the negative, adverbs are placed after the **pas**: **Elle dort bien.** *She sleeps well.* ➜ **Elle ne dort pas bien.** *She doesn't sleep well.*

10 **Put the words in the right order to form sentences.**

a. son / a / rapidement / bu / café / il
➜ ....

b. pas / au / cinéma / je / souvent / ne / vais
➜ ....

c. très / gentil / est / Sylvain / vraiment
➜ ....

d. sa / mieux / va / beaucoup / grand-mère
➜ ....

e. ne / Léa / mange / de / pain / jamais
➜ ....

f. au / ils / cinéma / sont / avant-hier / allés
➜ ....

Chouette! You've completed Lesson 17! It's time to count up the icons for the exercises and record your result here and in the table on page 127.

Making comparisons

The comparative and adjectives *(Le comparatif et les adjectifs)*

- The comparative is used to compare the qualities of two nouns. In English, this is often conveyed by adding the suffix *-er* to an adjective: *bigger*, *cheaper*, etc.
- In French, to express less than, **moins... que...** *less ... than* is placed around the adjective: **Karine est moins fatiguée que Coralie.** *Karine is less tired than Coralie.*
- To express the same as, **aussi... que...** *as ... as* is placed around the adjective: **Sophie est aussi intelligente qu'Éloïse.** *Sophie is as intelligent as Eloïse.*
- To express more than, **plus... que...** *more ... than* is placed around the adjective: **Pierre est plus bavard que Daniel.** *Pierre is more talkative than Daniel.*
- Note that **que** becomes **qu'** in front of a vowel or a silent **h**. Don't forget that an adjective must agree with the subject (i.e. the first of the two things compared).

More adjectives *(Autres adjectifs)*

The feminine form is shown in brackets.

affreux(se) [afruh(z)]	*awful*
amusant(e) [amewzah^{n}(t)]	*fun / funny*
difficile [deefeeseel]	*difficult*
ennuyeux(se) [ah^{n}new-ee-yuh(z)]	*boring*
facile [faseel]	*easy*
fatigant(e) [fateegah^{n}(t)]	*tiring*
fatigué(e) [fateegay]	*tired*
génial(e) [jzaynyal]	*great*
important(e) [a^{n}portah^{n}(t)]	*important*
intéressant(e) [a^{n}tehrehsah^{n}(t)]	*interesting*
inutile [eenewteel]	*useless*
mignon(ne) [meenyoh^{n}] / [meenyon]	*cute*
utile [ewteel]	*useful*

1 Match each French adjective to its English equivalent.

1. fatigué	**a.** useful
2. fatigant	**b.** cute
3. utile	**c.** funny
4. facile	**d.** boring
5. ennuyeux	**e.** tired
6. amusante	**f.** easy
7. mignonne	**g.** tiring

2 Write the feminine form of these adjectives and then translate them.

a. mignon ➜ .... ➜ ....
b. génial ➜ .... ➜ ....
c. intéressant ➜ .... ➜ ....
d. affreux ➜ .... ➜ ....
e. inutile ➜ .... ➜ ....
f. intelligent ➜ .... ➜ ....

3 Rewrite these sentences using comparative adjectives based on the symbols (- less than / = the same as / + more than).

E.g. La chimie est (utile =) le théâtre ➜ **La chimie est aussi utile que le théâtre.**

a. Les mathématiques sont (**utile +**) le sport. ➜ ....
b. L'histoire (f.) est (**intéressant -**) la chimie. ➜ ....
c. Le sport est (**amusant +**) le français. ➜ ....
d. La géographie est (**ennuyeux =**) la musique. ➜ ....
e. L'informatique (f.) est (**fatigant -**) le sport. ➜ ....

4 Translate these sentences into English.

a. La table est plus grande que la chaise. ➜ ....
....
b. Louis est moins gentil que Julian. ➜ ....
....
c. Le gâteau de Julie est aussi mauvais que le tien ! ➜ ....
....
d. Cette robe est plus jolie que celle-là *(that one)*. ➜ ....
....
e. Le sac bleu est aussi léger que le sac rouge. ➜ ....
....

The comparative and adverbs *(Le comparatif et les adverbes)*

With adverbs, the same rules apply as with adjectives when forming the comparative. **Il écrit <u>plus</u> lentement <u>qu</u>'elle.** *He writes <u>more</u> slowly <u>than</u> her.*

- As we saw on page 91, the most usual way to form an adverb is by adding the suffix **-ment** to an adjective. This suffix is added to a masculine adjective if the last letter is a vowel (**joli** *beautiful* ➔ **joliment** *beautifully*) or to the feminine form if it ends with a consonant (**seul** *sole* ➔ **seule** ➔ **seule<u>ment</u>** *solely, only*).
- There are also some irregular adverbs such as: **prudent** *careful* ➔ **prudemment** *carefully*, **énorme** *enormous* ➔ **énormément** *enormously*, **meilleur** *better* ➔ **mieux** *better*, **gentil** *kind* ➔ **gentiment** *kindly*.
- A few adverbs are not formed from adjectives: **vite** *quickly*, **bien** *well*, **mal** *badly*. **Je vais aussi vite que toi.** *I go as fast as you.* **L'élève parle moins bien que le professeur.** *The student doesn't speak as well as the teacher.*

5 Adjective or adverb? Place each word below into the right column.

gentil – mieux – lentement – mauvais
gentiment – doucement – jeune – heureuse

Adjectives	Adverbs

6 Turn these adjectives into adverbs.

a. rare ➔ ....

b. prudent ➔ ....

c. calme ➔ ....

d. rapide ➔ ....

e. énorme ➔ ....

f. gentil ➔ ....

The superlative *(Le superlatif)*

The superlative expresses the greatest degree of something in a comparison. In English, it is often formed by adding the suffix *-est* to an adjective or using *the most* or *the least* (e.g. *biggest*, *the most intelligent*, *the least expensive*, etc.).

- In French, the superlative is formed with a definite article (**le**, **la** or **les**) + **plus** *more* or **moins** *less* + adjective. The article and the adjective need to agree with the noun that they describe: **les pommes <u>les plus</u> rouges** *the reddest apples*.
- Note that the article used before the noun (**le, la** or **les**) should be the same as the article used in the superlative: **C'est <u>le</u> restaurant <u>le</u> plus cher de la ville.** *It's the most expensive restaurant in the city.*
- After a superlative, **de** is used to express *in*: **Martine est la plus intelligente de la classe.** *Martine is the smartest in the class.*

7 Circle the appropriate article.

a. C'est **le / la / les** plus belle maison du quartier *(neighbourhood)*.

b. C'est **le / la / les** plus gentil professeur de l'école.

c. Ce sont les garçons **le / la / les** plus polis *(polite)* de la classe.

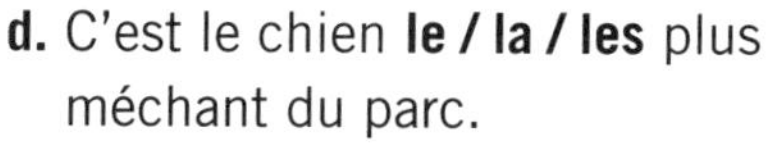

d. C'est le chien **le / la / les** plus méchant du parc.

e. C'est la robe **le / la / les** plus jolie du magasin.

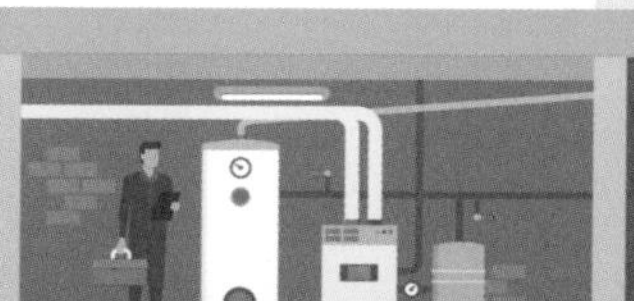

8 Write the correct form of the adjective.

E.g. Ces bébés sont les plus (mignon) de l'hôpital. → **mignons**

a. Ce film est le plus (**intéressant**) de la collection. → ....

b. Ces paniers *(baskets)* sont les plus (**lourd**) du marché. → ....

c. Leurs voitures sont les plus (**propre** *clean*) de la rue ! → ....

d. Ces filles sont les plus (**gentil**) de la famille. → ....

e. Cette grand-mère est la plus (**vieux**) du village. → ....

Irregular forms *(Formes irrégulières)*

There are some adjectives that have specific forms in the comparative or superlative.

- The adjective **mauvais** *bad* becomes **pire** *worse* in the comparative (and not **le plus mauvais**!): **Il est pire que moi.** *He is worse than me.* In the superlative it becomes **le/la/les pire(s)** *the worst*: **C'est la pire semaine de ma vie !** *It's the worst week of my life!*
- The adjective **bon** *good* becomes **meilleur** *better* in the comparative and **le/la/les meilleur** *the best* in the superlative.
- The adverb **bien** *well* becomes **mieux** *better* in the comparative: **Je me sens mieux depuis la semaine dernière.** *I'm feeling better since last week.*

9 Write the appropriate comparative or superlative form.

E.g. Noah est (+ mignon) **le plus mignon** de sa classe.

a. C'est **(+ bon)** dessert .... du menu.

b. Elles sont **(+ timide)** .... leurs sœurs.

c. Audrey est **(+ généreuse)** .... de la famille.

d. Ce film est **(+ mauvais)** .... du programme.

e. Lola est **(+ jeune)** .... Vanessa.

10 Translate these sentences into French.

a. This book is the worst ('book') in the library.

→ ....

....

b. Davy is smaller than Geoffrey.

→ ....

....

c. Edwige is the happiest girl in the school.

→ ....

....

d. Ninon is not as sad as ('is less sad than') Olivier.

→ ....

....

e. These boys are the best players (**joueurs**) on the team (**l'équipe**).

→ ....

....

Well done! You've completed Lesson 18! It's time to count up the icons for the exercises and record your result here and on page 127.

Linking words

Conjunctions *(Les conjonctions)*

Conjunctions, or linking words, are used to connect words, phrases or sentences. They include words such as **et** *and*, **mais** *but*, **ou** *or* and **parce que** *because*.

Coordinating conjunctions *(Les conjonctions de coordination)*

A coordinating conjunction is used to link two elements of equal importance.

d'ailleurs [da-yuhr]	*for that matter*
ainsi [a^{n}see]	*thus*
au contraire [oh koh^{n}trehr]	*on the contrary*
aussi [ohsee]	*so, also*
car [kar]	*because*
c'est-à-dire [sehtadeer]	*that's to say*
c'est pourquoi [seh poorkwa]	*that's why*
cependant [suhpah^{n}dah^n]	*however, nevertheless*
donc [doh^{n}k]	*so, therefore, consequently*

en effet [ah^n nehfeh]	*indeed*
et [eh]	*and*
mais [meh]	*but*
néanmoins [nay-ah^{n}mwa^n]	*nevertheless*
ni... ni... [nee nee]	*neither ... nor*
or [or]	*however*
ou [oo]	*or*
pourtant [poortah^n]	*however*
toutefois [tootfwa]	*however*
soit... soit... [swa swa]	*either ... or ....*

a. Je l'ai attendu *(waited for him)* mais il n'est pas venu.

b. Ni Sophie ni Loïc n'ont de chien.

c. J'ai faim *(I'm hungry)*. Toutefois, je t'attendrai pour manger.

d. Il fait très froid aujourd'hui ; d'ailleurs, nous avons mis le chauffage *(heating)*.

e. Il pleut beaucoup donc j'ai pris le parapluie *(umbrella)*.

f. Tu viens avec moi ou tu restes *(stay)* à la maison ?

 Complete the sentences with the appropriate conjunction below. 

soit... soit... - donc - c'est pourquoi - et - car

a. Laetitia n'aime pas skier, ... elle reste au chalet.

b. Je suis au lit .... je suis malade *(ill)*.

c. .... Lucien .... Christophe a un bateau *(boat)*.

d. Lauriane s'est levée .... elle a pris son petit déjeuner.

e. Charlie n'a pas réussi son examen ; .... il est grognon *(grumpy)*.

Subordinating conjunctions *(Les conjonctions de subordination)*

These are used to link a subordinate clause to a main clause. A subordinate (or dependent) clause is a phrase that gives more information about the main clause. It is typically introduced by a conjunction. While the main clause can stand alone, a subordinate clause only makes sense in the context of the main clause it modifies.

Main clause	Subordinate clause
Je l'aime bien	**parce qu'elle est très gentille.**
I like her a lot	*because she is very kind.*

Subordinating conjunctions *(Les conjonctions de subordination)*

alors que [alor kuh]	*while*
à moins que [a mwa^{n} kuh]	*unless*
afin que [afa^{n} kuh]	*in order that, so that*
après que [apreh kuh]	*after*
aussitôt que [ohseetoh kuh]	*as soon as*
comme [kom]	*as, since*
depuis que [duhpew-ee kuh]	*since*

dès que [day kuh]	*as soon as*
lorsque [lorskuh]	*when*
parce que [parsuh kuh]	*because*
pendant que [pah^{n}dah^{n} kuh]	*while*
puisque [pew-eesk]	*since*
quand [kah^{n}]	*when*
que [kuh]	*that*
si [see]	*if*
tandis que [tah^{n}dee kuh]	*while, whereas*

Note: these conjunctions are followed by verbs in the indicative (as opposed to the subjunctive), which is the grammatical mood we have been learning in this workbook.

3 Match the French conjunction to its English equivalent.

1. pendant que	**a.** when
2. lorsque	**b.** as, because
3. tandis que	**c.** since, ever since
4. aussitôt que	**d.** while, during
5. après que	**e.** after
6. depuis que	**f.** whereas
7. comme	**g.** as soon as

4 Underline the subordinating conjunctions and then translate them.

a. Je suis tombé amoureux *(I fell in love)* d'Ophélie dès que je l'ai vue.
➜ ....

b. Mathilde est en colère *(angry)* parce que son chien a mangé le gâteau.
➜ ....

c. Quand il rentre de l'école, il mange beaucoup.
➜ ....

d. Je ne cuisine *(cook)* pas de brocolis puisque les enfants ne les aiment pas.
➜ ....

e. Si tu veux plus de chocolat, tu dois demander !
➜ ....

f. Depuis que je suis allée au Portugal, je veux y retourner *(to go back there)* !
➜ ....

Other conjunctions *(Autres conjonctions)*

The table on the next page lists a variety of different conjunctions and linking words that can be used when constructing sentences. These allow you to show chronology, suggest an alternative, contrast opposing ideas, offer examples, or make a concluding statement.

Showing chronology or sequence *(Ordonner)*

d'abord [dabor]	*first*
premièrement [pruhmee-ehrmah^n]	*firstly*
deuxièmement [duhzee-ehmmah^n]	*secondly*
ensuite [ah^{n}sew-eet] / **puis** [pew-ee]	*then*
finalement [feenalmah^n]	*finally*

Suggesting an alternative *(Proposer une alternative)*

d'un côté [da^n kohtay] **...** **de l'autre** [duh lohtr] **...**	*on the one hand ...* *on the other ...*
ou ... ou ... [oo]	*either ... or ...*
par ailleurs [par a-yuhr] **de plus** [duh plews]	*moreover*

Contrasting opposing ideas *(Opposer des idées)*

au contraire [oh koh^{n}trehr]	*on the contrary*
par contre [par koh^{n}tr] **d'un autre côté** [da^n nohtr kohtay]	*on the other hand*
en revanche [ah^n ruhvah^{n}sh]	*in contrast*

Giving examples *(Suggérer des exemples)*

ainsi [a^{n}see]	*thus*
donc [doh^{n}k]	*therefore, so*
notamment [notamah^n]	*particularly /* *in particular*
par exemple [par egzah^{n}pl]	*for example*

Concluding *(Conclure)*

en bref [ah^n brehf]	*in short*
en conclusion [ah^n koh^{n}klewzyoh^n] **pour conclure** [poor koh^{n}klewr]	*to conclude*
en résumé [ah^n rayzewmay]	*to sum up*
finalement [feenalmah^n]	*finally*
pour finir [poor feeneer]	*to end*

1. notamment	a. thus
2. pour finir	b. for example
3. ainsi	c. on the other hand
4. ensuite	d. particularly
5. par exemple	e. in short
6. en résumé	f. finally
7. par contre	g. then

6 Fill in the blanks using the appropriate words below.

finalement – deuxièmement – de plus – ensuite
en résumé – premièrement – par contre

« Mon voyage en Italie est un vrai désastre ! (a) ...., le train était très en retard (very late). (b) ...., j'ai perdu un sac ! (c) ...., le train s'est arrêté pendant une heure. (d) ...., nous sommes arrivés à Florence avec trois heures de retard. (e) ...., il fait très chaud en Italie, c'est affreux. (f) ...., les Italiens sont très sympas (very nice) et la nourriture (food) est délicieuse ! (g) ...., un voyage agréable (pleasant) mais parfois frustrant (frustrating) ! »

7 Complete the sentences with the appropriate conjunction.

a. Je ne suis pas allée au cinéma .... je n'aime pas le film.

b. Luc n'aime pas les chats. ...., il en a adopté un ! Il s'appelle Tigrou.

c. .... l'automne arrive, les feuilles *(the leaves)* tombent.

d. .... tu veux acheter une nouvelle console de jeu *(game console)*, économise ton argent de poche *(save your pocket money)* !

e. Louise est fatiguée, ... elle veut aller à la fête !

f. Patrice déteste les fruits : ...., il ne peut pas manger d'oranges.

Splendide ! You've reached the end of Lesson 19! It's time to count up the icons for the exercises and record your result here and on page 127.

1 Write these numbers in French.

a. 10 ....

b. 54 ....

c. 100 ....

d. 205 ....

e. 6 ....

f. 25 ....

g. 589 ....

h. 999 ....

2 Translate the following sentences into French.

a. My father is in the attic. ➜ ....

....

b. Her brothers are in the kitchen. ➜ ....

....

c. His parents are lawyers. ➜ ....

....

d. Her grandmother is a dentist. ➜ ....

....

e. Your (informal sing.) sister is in the bathroom. ➜ ....

....

f. Your (pl.) mother is a teacher. ➜ ....

....

Label each picture with the correct French term and definite article.

a. ....

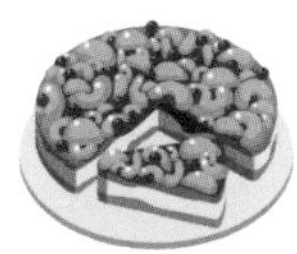

b. ....

c. ....

d. ....

e. ....

f. ....

g. ....

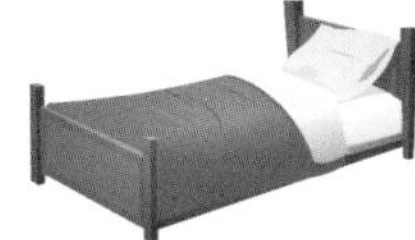

h. ....

i. ....

j. ....

k. ....

l. ....

4 Find the French equivalents of these adjectives in the grid.

small
old
young
difficult
pretty
happy x 2

A	C	E	G	J	Q	A	E	V	E
D	F	M	H	L	P	E	T	I	T
E	J	O	L	I	M	A	D	E	R
D	R	C	C	M	L	J	U	U	F
I	D	H	E	U	R	E	U	X	D
F	D	E	B	B	Z	U	Z	W	C
F	V	A	F	B	U	N	D	V	X
I	D	G	H	V	T	E	B	E	G
C	N	E	E	H	I	F	E	R	T
I	L	I	U	G	L	É	G	E	R
L	O	U	R	D	E	J	A	W	I
E	O	A	E	R	S	G	E	T	S
B	M	A	U	V	A	I	S	H	T
S	A	C	X	D	U	P	E	F	E

ugly
sad
heavy
light
useful
bad

5 **Unscramble the letters to find these adjectives of nationality, then write the name of the corresponding country with article.**

E.g. icmaaerin → **américain → les États-Unis**

a. dleaalnm → .... → ....

b. iishonc → .... → ....

c. issseu → .... → ....

d. lesnapgo → .... → ....

e. aaspojni → .... → ....

f. séenrialnda → .... → ....

6 **Match these animals to the English equivalents and then write the corresponding indefinite article.**

1. .... chat

2. .... serpent

3. .... chevaux

4. .... lapine

5. .... tortue

6. .... souris

7. .... chienne

a. a snake

b. some horses

c. a mouse

d. a cat

e. a (female) rabbit

f. a (female) dog

g. a turtle

7 **Write the times.**

a. 2.15 = Il est ....

b. 15.25 = Il est ....

c. 20.45 = Il est ....

d. 8.30 = Il est ....

e. 16.10 = Il est ....

f. 5.55 = Il est ....

8 Conjugate the following verbs in the present tense.

écouter *to listen*	**finir** *to finish*	**vendre** *to sell*
je/j'	je/j'	je/j' ....
tu	tu	tu ....
il/elle	il/elle	il/elle ....
nous	nous	nous ....
vous	vous	vous ....
ils/elles	ils/elles	ils/elles ....
être *to be*	**avoir** *to have*	**aller** *to go*
je/j'	je/j'	je/j' ....
tu	tu	tu ....
il/elle	il/elle	il/elle ....
nous	nous	nous ....
vous	vous	vous ....
ils/elles	ils/elles	ils/elles ....
appeler *to call*	**prendre** *to take*	**faire** *to do, to make*
je/j'	je/j'	je/j' ....
tu	tu	tu ....
il/elle	il/elle	il/elle ....
nous	nous	nous ....
vous	vous	vous ....
ils/elles	ils/elles	ils/elles ....

9 Write the question that corresponds to each answer.

a. .... ? – Je m'appelle Amélie.

b. .... ? – J'habite à Paris.

c. .... ? – Antoine va au musée avec moi.

d. .... ? – Sophie vient demain.

e. .... ? – J'ai neuf chemises.

f. .... ? – Je suis fatiguée parce que je me suis couchée à minuit.

10 Use these elements to form complete sentences.

E.g. Ethan / 1 / grey / coat ➜ **Ethan a un manteau gris.**

a. Léo / 5 / black / trousers ➜ ....

b. Bérénice / 10 / pink / hats ➜ ....

c. Maël / 20 / green / caps ➜ ....

d. Sasha / 0 / red / dress ➜ ....

e. Colin and Marie / 3 / brown / shirts ➜ ....

f. You / 7 / purple / pyjamas ➜ ....

11 Translate these past tense sentences into French using the present perfect.

a. Caroline went to the cinema yesterday. ➜ ....

b. Francis ate the strawberries. ➜ ....

c. I have read all the books. ➜ ....

d. They loved this museum. ➜ ....

e. You did your homework. ➜ ....

f. They sold their house. ➜ ....

12 **Use the prompts to write two sentences as shown in the example.**
☺ = aimer ☺☺ = adorer ☹ = ne pas aimer ☹☹ = détester

E.g. Tom ☹ cycling → **Tom n'aime pas le cyclisme. / Tom n'aime pas faire du vélo.**

a. Chantal and Clément / ☺☺ / swimming

→ ....

→ ....

b. You (informal sing.) / ☹ / tennis

→ ....

→ ....

c. I / ☺ / walking

→ ....

→ ....

d. We / ☹☹ / gymnastics

→ ....

→ ....

e. Manon / ☺ / rugby

→ ....

→ ....

13 **Place the missing accents and other diacritical marks on these words.**

a. Noel

b. Paques

c. une fete

d. francais

e. zero

f. aout

g. ta mere

h. une secretaire

i. une lecon

j. bientot

k. un velo

l. un hotel

m. vous etes

n. americain

o. les pates

14 **Tick whether the following words are masculine (M) or feminine (F) and if they are plural (P).**

	M	F	P
a. ma sœur			
b. la viande			
c. une fermière			
d. mes frères			
e. l'eau			
f. des musiciens			
g. un dentiste			
h. l'orange (*the fruit*)			
i. mon grand-père			
j. les pommes de terre			

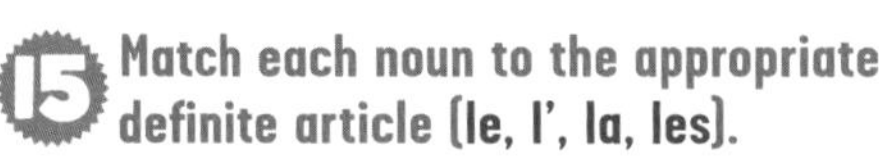

15 **Match each noun to the appropriate definite article (le, l', la, les).**

le •

l' •

la •

les •

• *salon*
• *toilettes*
• *chambres*
• *hôtel*
• *garage*
• *salle à manger*
• *entrée (entrance)*
• *cuisine*

16 Write the feminine form of each of these adjectives.

a. Il est joli. ➜ Elle est ....

b. Il est heureux. ➜ Elle est ....

c. Il est léger. ➜ Elle est ....

d. Il est grand. ➜ Elle est ....

e. Il est canadien. ➜ Elle est ....

f. Il est vieux. ➜ Elle est ....

g. Il est bon. ➜ Elle est ....

h. Il est amoureux. ➜ Elle est ....

17 Underline the correct possessive adjective.

a. Regarde ! **Ta / Mon / Ses** chat dort sur le canapé !

b. Elle aime beaucoup **ta / mon / ses** frères.

c. Connais-tu *(Do you know)* **sa / mon / leurs** amie Lucile ?

d. Vous devez visiter **ma / ton / ses** nouvelle maison !

e. Où est **mon / tes / ta** raquette de tennis ?

f. Elle a perdu **ma / ton / leurs** clés.

18 Complete each sentence with the correct subject pronoun.

a. .... regardons la télévision avec Laurent et Sophie.

b. .... ai mangé trop de bonbons !

c. .... embrasse tous les garçons de l'école !

d. Es- .... allé à la poste ce matin ?

e. .... réussissez toujours vos tests ?

f. .... aiment aller au cinéma le samedi soir.

19 Complete each sentence using the correct direct or indirect object pronoun.

a. Ils .... écoutent. (to me)

b. Tu .... attends ? (for us)

c. Je .... demande demain. ([to] him)

d. Nous .... invitons bientôt. (you, pl.)

e. Vous .... téléphonez demain ? ([to] her)

f. Elle .... aime beaucoup. (you, informal sing.)

g. Sarah .... répond. ([to] them)

20 Write these ordinal numbers as words (e.g. 1er **premier**).

a. 4e ....

b. 20e ....

c. 14e ....

d. 32e ....

e. 100e ....

f. 60e ....

g. 12e ....

21 Conjugate these reflexive verbs in the future tense.

a. Nous **(se laver)** .... à 8 heures demain matin.

b. Renaud **(s'habiller)** .... très vite car il est en retard.

c. Adèle et Mathilde **(se lever)** .... à 7 h 30 jeudi prochain.

d. Tu **(se brosser)** .... les dents ce soir.

e. Vous **(se réveiller)** .... à 10 heures ce week-end.

f. Je **(se promener)** .... dans le jardin plus tard.

Congratulations! You've completed all of the exercises in this workbook! It's time to count up the icons for this review and record your result here and in the final table on page 127.

1. Alphabet & pronunciation

1 **a.** Martine: em-ah-air-tay-ee-en-uh **b.** Xavier: eeks-ah-vay-ee-uh-air **c.** Gilles: zhay-ee-el-el-uh-es **d.** Joseph: zhee-oh-es-uh-pay-ash **e.** Patrick: pay-ah-tay-air-ee-say-kah

2 monsieur *sir* – au revoir *goodbye* – bonjour *good morning* (also *hello*) – bonne nuit *good night* – salut *hi* – mademoiselle *miss* – à bientôt *see you soon*

3 **a.** salut *hi* **b.** bonsoir *good evening* **c.** madame *madam* **d.** bientôt *soon* **e.** bienvenue *welcome*

4 **a.** Pâques: pay-ah[accent circonflexe]-kew-ew-uh-es **b.** Noël: en-oh-uh[tréma]-el **c.** Pentecôte: pay-uh-en-tay-uh-say-oh[accent circonflexe]-tay-uh **d.** Épiphanie: uh[accent aigu]-pay-ee-pay-ash-ah-en-ee-uh **e.** pères: pay-uh[accent grave]-air-uh-es

5 **a.** âge *age* **b.** être *to be* **c.** frère *brother* **d.** salut *hi* **e.** France **f.** français *French* **g.** fête *celebration, holiday*

6 **a.** père *father* **b.** août *August* **c.** leçon *lesson* **d.** Suède *Sweden* **e.** canoë *canoe* **f.** américain *American*

7 estomac = estohmah; salut = sahlew; abricot = ahbreekoh; nerf = nehr; trop = troh; deux = duh; outil = ootee; trois = trwah; mot = moh; froid = frwah

8 deux – 2; dix – 10; zéro – 0; neuf – 9; cinq – 5; huit – 8; sept – 7

10

	1	2	3	4	5	6	7	8	9	10	11	12	13
A					T	R	O	I	S				
B									A/Â	G	E		
C					M				L				
D				B	O	N	J	O	U	R		M	
E					N				T			È	
F			D		S			C		Z	É	R	O
G	A	M	E	R	I	C	A	I	N			E	U
H	M		U		E			N	E	U	F		T
I	I		X		U	N		Q			R		I
J					R					N	O	Ë	L
K											I		
L											D	I	X

2. More on pronunciation

1 **a.** salut *hi* **b.** ami *friend* **c.** mère *mother* **d.** quatre *four* **e.** mot *word* **f.** américain *American*

2 **a.** zéro *zero* **b.** quatorze *fourteen* **c.** huit *eight* **d.** dix-neuf *nineteen* **e.** vingt *twenty* **f.** treize *thirteen*

3 **a.** onze [oh^n] **b.** à demain [a^n] **c.** tante [ah^n] **d.** faim [a^n] **e.** chacun [a^n] **f.** bonjour [oh^n] **g.** patin [a^n] **h.** parfum [a^n]

4 **a.** sœur *sister* **b.** douze *twelve* **c.** grand-père *grandfather* **d.** enfant *child* **e.** cinq *five* **f.** oncle *uncle*

5 **a.** [tew] **b.** [salew] **c.** [mewzeek] **d.** [bews] **e.** [flewt]

6 **a.** [tewtew] **b.** [toot] **c.** [jzoor] **d.** [fewtewr] **e.** [dooz]

7 **a.** [boh^{n}jzoor] **b.** [trwa] **c.** [oh ruhvwar] **d.** [katr] **e.** [ehtr]

8 mère = Martine; sœur = Audrey; père = Guy; grand-mère = Michelle; frère = Alexandre; grand-père = Marcel

3. Nouns & articles

1 mère (f.); chambre (f.); fils (m.); salon (m.); grenier (m.); maison (f.)

2 **a.** salon *living room* **b.** maison *house* **c.** garage *garage* **d.** cuisine *kitchen* **e.** chambre *bedroom* **f.** grenier *attic*

3 **a.** des greniers **b.** des sœurs **c.** des salons **d.** des parfums **e.** des chambres **f.** des pères

4 **a.** W **b.** M **c.** W **d.** W/M **e.** W/M **f.** M **g.** M

5 **a.** Nous sommes musiciennes. **b.** Nous sommes médecins. **c.** Nous sommes dentistes. **d.** Nous sommes bouchères. **e.** Nous sommes chanteuses.

6 **a.** f. **b.** m./f. **c.** m./f. **d.** f. **e.** f.

7 **a.** une **b.** un **c.** des **d.** la **e.** le **f.** les **g.** *Je suis / Nous sommes* **h.** There is no article in front of one's occupation in French.

8 **a.** La **b.** Les **c.** Le **d.** Les **e.** Les **f.** La

9 **a.** cuisine **b.** garçons **c.** avocat **d.** comédien

10 je suis – tu es – il/elle est – nous sommes – vous êtes – ils/elles sont

11 j'ai – tu as – il/elle a – nous avons – vous avez – ils/elles ont

12 **1.** d **2.** f **3.** a **4.** e **5.** c **6.** b

4. Pronouns & more on articles

1 **a.** des **b.** un **c.** un **d.** une **e.** un

2 **a.** une **b.** une **c.** des **d.** des **e.** des **f.** un **g.** des **h.** un **i.** des

3 **a.** FS **b.** FP **c.** MS **d.** MS **e.** FS **f.** MP **g.** FS

4 **a.** de la **b.** du **c.** des **d.** de la **e.** des **f.** du **g.** de la **h.** de l'

5 **a.** du gâteau **b.** des bonbons **c.** du lait **d.** de la tomate **e.** de la viande **f.** des pâtes

6 **1.** f **2.** e **3.** b **4.** c **5.** d **6.** a

7 elle *she*; nous *we*; je/j' *I*; ils *they* (m.); vous *you* (pl. & formal); il *he*; tu *you* (informal sing.); elles *they* (f.)

8 **a.** Je **b.** Nous **c.** Vous **d.** Elles **e.** Il **f.** J'

9 te/t' *you* (informal sing.); le/l' *him/it*; vous *you* (formal / plural); nous *us*; me/m' *me*; les *them*; la/l' *her/it*

10 **a.** m' **b.** les **c.** la **d.** t' **e.** nous **f.** l'

11 **a.** m' **b.** vous **c.** leur **d.** lui **e.** lui

5. Adjectives

1 **a.** jolie **b.** petite **c.** lourde **d.** vieille **e.** méchante **f.** jeune

2 **a.** lourds **b.** grandes **c.** légers **d.** tristes **e.** fous **f.** moches

3 vieille – jeune; petits – grands; gentilles – méchantes; moche – belle; heureuse – triste; lourde – légère; bons – mauvais

4 **a.** jolis **b.** heureux **c.** grandes **d.** mauvais **e.** petite **f.** belles **g.** bonne **h.** vieux

5 **1.** violet **2.** violette **3.** violettes **4.** verte **5.** verts **6.** vertes **7.** bleu **8.** bleue **9.** bleus **10.** orange **11.** orange **12.** orange **13.** gris **14.** grise **15.** grises **16.** blanc **17.** blancs **18.** blanches **19.** noir **20.** noire **21.** noirs **22.** rouge **23.** rouges **24.** rouges **25.** marron **26.** marron **27.** marron **28.** rose **29.** roses **30.** roses

6 **a.** verte **b.** violets **c.** blanches **d.** noir **e.** bleues

7 **a.** The table is green. **b.** The sofas are purple. **c.** The chairs are white. **d.** The desk is black. **e.** The bedside tables are blue.

8 **1.** Hollandaise **2.** Espagnol **3.** Italien **4.** Italiens **5.** Japonaise **6.** Japonaises **7.** Allemand **8.** Allemande **9.** Allemands **10.** Suisse **11.** Suisses **12.** Suisses **13.** Australiens **14.** Australiennes

9

F	C	V	T	D	H	A	L	N	A
S	E	H	D	O	I	S	O	A	C
E	A	O	L	C	D	D	N	M	N
N	N	L	V	B	E	L	G	E	N
N	G	L	E	J	N	E	A	R	E
E	L	A	S	A	H	S	P	I	I
I	A	N	O	P	I	L	S	C	L
D	I	D	E	O	C	S	E	A	A
A	S	A	N	N	S	U	T	I	R
N	D	I	T	A	L	I	E	N	T
A	H	S	N	I	A	S	I	E	S
C	S	D	E	S	D	S	F	D	U
N	A	D	N	A	M	E	L	L	A

6. Possession & likes and dislikes

1 **a.** sa souris **b.** leur sœur **c.** C'est ton cheval. **d.** C'est notre grand-père. **e.** C'est votre poisson. **f.** vos chiens

2 **a.** mes **b.** ta **c.** vos **d.** son **e.** notre **f.** leur

3 **a.** le poisson *the fish* **b.** la souris *the mouse* **c.** le serpent *the snake* **d.** le cheval *the horse* **e.** la lapine *the rabbit* (female) **f.** le hamster *the hamster*

4 **a.** j' **b.** -e **c.** group – polite/formal

5 **a.** j'adore **b.** tu adores **c.** il/elle adore **d.** nous adorons **e.** vous adorez **f.** ils/elles adorent

6

F	R	O	P	S	H	Y	U	F	P	M
Y	J	E	M	N	J	U	D	O	U	i
K	L	N	A	T	A	T	i	O	N	M
A	W	F	R	R	T	E	O	T	A	A
i	R	A	C	Q	E	P	O	B	T	S
S	U	T	H	A	N	D	B	A	L	L
S	G	U	E	E	N	R	T	L	J	i
H	B	M	D	S	i	Y	G	L	D	L
C	Y	C	L	i	S	M	E	B	H	M

walking marche; *handball* handball; *football* football; *rugby* rugby; *cycling* cyclisme; *swimming* natation; *judo* judo

7 **a.** Julien loves playing tennis. **b.** Coralie and Sidonie hate football. **c.** We like running. **d.** You (pl. or formal) love doing gymnastics. **e.** They (m. or mixed gender) like playing handball.

8 **a.** Nous détestons le rugby. / Nous détestons jouer au rugby. **b.** Karine et Lucie adorent la natation. / Karine et Lucie adorent nager. **c.** Tu aimes le cyclisme. / Tu aimes faire du vélo. **d.** Je déteste le judo. / Je déteste faire du judo. **e.** Vous adorez la marche. / Vous adorez marcher.

9 **a.** a and c **b.** b and d **c.** **ne** + **pas** around the verb **d.** The **ne** becomes **n'** in front of a vowel.

10 **a.** Je n'aime pas les bonbons. **b.** Je n'écoute pas ta mère. **c.** Il ne parle pas beaucoup. **d.** Elles ne regardent pas la télévision. **e.** Vous n'aidez pas votre sœur.

11 **a.** la jupe **b.** la casquette **c.** les chaussettes **d.** le pyjama **e.** la chemise

12 **a.** Ces **b.** Cette **c.** Ce **d.** Ce **e.** Cette

7. The present tense

1 **a.** J' **b.** Vous **c.** Elles **d.** Nous **e.** Tu

2 **a.** regarde **b.** jouons **c.** téléphone **d.** aidez **e.** appellent

3 **a.** parles **b.** joue **c.** aimons **d.** regardent **e.** demandez **f.** écoute

4 **a.** finit **b.** bâtissons **c.** choisissez **d.** réussis **e.** nourrissent **f.** réfléchis

5 **a.** choisis **b.** finissez **c.** nourris **d.** remplissent **e.** réfléchissons

6 **a.** choisis **b.** finissez **c.** remplit **d.** réussissons **e.** réfléchissent

7 **a.** Je/Tu **b.** Nous **c.** Vous **d.** Ils/Elles **e.** Il/Elle

8 1–e; 2–a; 3–f; 4–c; 5–d; 6–b

9 **a.** They sell / are selling their house. **b.** We are succeeding in making our cake **c.** You (pl. or formal) choose / are choosing a name for the cat. **d.** I lose / am losing my books. **e.** She kisses / is kissing Pacôme. **f.** You help / are helping Romain

⑩ **a.** Ils finissent le dîner. **b.** Je réussis à la natation. **c.** Nous descendons de cheval. **d.** Elle entend le chien. **e.** Tu donnes ton manteau. **f.** Vous demandez une table.

8. Numbers & time

❶

E	R	T	A	U	Q	E	T	N	A	X	I	O	S
Q	D	R	C	E	Q	U	A	R	A	N	T	E	K
H	V	V	E	N	Q	O	U	D	R	L	E	T	M
A	C	I	N	Q	U	A	N	T	E	D	E	U	X
E	J	N	T	F	I	O	U	M	R	S	A	I	S
T	N	G	T	I	N	M	S	I	T	O	X	M	K
P	M	T	U	E	Z	I	E	R	T	Z	I	W	P
E	S	D	S	R	E	L	Y	A	C	J	S	S	O
S	O	E	B	O	T	L	R	M	I	I	G	G	R
F	Q	U	A	T	R	E	V	I	N	G	T	U	N
D	I	X	G	Z	E	C	X	U	Q	Y	A	C	T
O	A	F	U	E	N	A	P	D	U	A	O	V	M
U	R	H	U	I	T	T	O	B	A	Z	E	R	O
Z	U	I	S	K	E	R	I	F	N	R	U	S	O
E	B	O	M	A	Z	Q	U	A	T	O	R	Z	E
I	U	S	O	I	X	A	N	T	E	D	I	X	A

0 = zéro, 3 = trois, 7 = sept, 8 = huit, 9 = neuf, 10 = dix, 12 = douze, 13 = treize, 14 = quatorze, 15 = quinze, 22 = vingt-deux, 30 = trente, 40 = quarante, 50 = cinquante, 52 = cinquante-deux, 64 = soixante-quatre, 70 = soixante-dix, 81 = quatre-vingt-un, 100 = cent, 1 000 = mille

❷ **a.** douze **b.** trente **c.** soixante-dix **d.** quarante et un **e.** quarante-cinq **f.** trente-deux

❸ **a.** quarante-sept **b.** vingt-deux **c.** mille **d.** quatre-vingts **e.** quatorze **f.** soixante

❹ **a.** 3ᵉ **b.** 1000ᵉ **c.** 70ᵉ **d.** 16ᵉ **e.** 60ᵉ **f.** 19ᵉ **g.** 91ᵉ

❺ **a.** premier **b.** quatorzième **c.** vingtième **d.** trente-deuxième **e.** cinquante-cinquième **f.** soixante-huitième **g.** quatre-vingt-sixième **h.** centième

❻ **a.** premier/première **b.** douzième **c.** cinquantième **d.** centième **e.** dix-septième **f.** neuvième **g.** cinquante-deuxième

❼

❽ **a.** Il est trois heures / quinze heures. **b.** Il est minuit / midi. **c.** Il est neuf heures et demie / vingt et une heures trente. **d.** Il est onze heures et quart / vingt-trois heures quinze. **e.** Il est six heures moins le quart / dix-sept heures quarante-cinq. **f.** Il est huit heures / vingt heures.

❾ 22:25 → dix heures vingt-cinq; 8:40 → neuf heures moins vingt; 5:10 → cinq heures dix; 12:00 → midi; 15:45 → quatre heures moins le quart; 6:50 → sept heures moins dix

9. More on the present tense

❶ **a.** espérons **b.** achètes **c.** commencez **d.** envoient **e.** rangeons

❷ **a.** mangeons **b.** jette **c.** préfèrent **d.** appelles **e.** nettoie

❸ appeler → c; jeter → a; manger → f; acheter → b; envoyer → e; nettoyer → d

❹ **1.** b or e **2.** b or e **3.** f **4.** a **5.** c **6.** d

❺ **a.** I/you have to drink water. **b.** I/you say goodbye to your grandmother. **c.** She puts on her blue dress. **d.** We are painting the living room's wall. **e.** You are making a chocolate cake. **f.** They read a lot of books.

❻ **a.** crois **b.** lisez **c.** peuvent **d.** savons **e.** dois

❼ **a.** me **b.** se **c.** nous **d.** te **e.** vous

❽ **a.** s' **b.** nous **c.** m' **d.** se **e.** vous **f.** te

❾ **a.** se couche **b.** nous promenons **c.** me lave **d.** s'habillent **e.** te réveilles

❿ **a.** la bouche *the mouth* **b.** les oreilles *the ears* **c.** les mains *the hands* **d.** les cheveux *the hair* **e.** les jambes *the legs* **f.** le ventre *the stomach*

10. More on pronouns

❶ **1.** c/d **2.** b/e **3.** f **4.** c/d **5.** b/e **6.** a

❷ **a.** J'adore ces chapeaux mais je veux celui-ci. **b.** J'adore ces chaussettes mais je veux celles-là. **c.** J'adore ces chemises mais je veux celle-là. **d.** J'adore ces jupes mais je veux celles-ci. **e.** J'adore ces casquettes mais je veux celle-ci.

❸ **a.** le leur **b.** les siens **c.** la vôtre **d.** le mien **e.** la sienne **f.** les tiennes

❹ **a.** le nôtre **b.** la tienne **c.** les vôtres **d.** les miennes **e.** le sien **f.** les leurs

❺ **a.** un bâton de colle (*a glue stick*) **b.** un tableau (*a board*) **c.** des ciseaux (*scissors*) **d.** un livre (*a book*) **e.** une gomme (*a rubber or an eraser*)

❻ **1.** c **2.** f **3.** e **4.** a **5.** d **6.** b

❼ **a.** quels **b.** quelle **c.** quelles **d.** lesquels **e.** laquelle **f.** lesquelles

❽ **a.** Quel **b.** Lesquelles **c.** Quels **d.** Laquelle / Lesquelles **e.** Quelle **f.** Lequel / Lesquels

11. Types of sentences

❶

	Subject	Verb	Complement
a)	il	travaille	dans sa chambre
b)	nous	aimons	jouer au football
c)	elle	aide	sa mère
d)	vous	détestez	les mathématiques
e)	tu	adores	l'anglais

❷ **a.** Elle embrasse ton cousin. **b.** Nous aimons la robe bleue. **c.** Vous téléphonez à votre grand-père. **d.** Loïc aime les vacances en Australie. **e.** Carole et Clothilde choisissent les chaussures rouges.

❸ **a.** la chimie **b.** l'informatique **c.** le français **d.** le sport **e.** l'histoire **f.** le dessin

❹ **a.** Je n'aime pas les pommes vertes. **b.** Elles ne sont jamais tristes. **c.** Carlos n'a aucun film en anglais. **d.** Louis et Suzanne ne jouent plus au basket-ball. **e.** Tu n'es ni grand ni petit.

❺ **a.** I don't like green apples. **b.** They (f.) are never sad. **c.** Carlos doesn't have any films in English. **d.** Louis and Suzanne no longer play basketball. **e.** You are neither tall nor short.

❻ **a.** Camille n'aime pas le chocolat. **b.** Pascal ne regarde pas la télé. **c.** Je n'ai aucun chapeau bleu. **d.** Ella ne mange jamais de tomates. **e.** Ma sœur n'a ni jupe ni robe / ni robe ni jupe.

❼ **a.** Camille doesn't like chocolate. **b.** Pascal doesn't watch / is not watching TV. **c.** I don't have a blue hat / any blue hats. **d.** Ella never eats tomatoes. **e.** My sister has neither a skirt nor a dress / a dress nor a skirt.

❽ **a.** As-tu un chat ? / Tu as un chat ? **b.** Aime-t-elle les croissants ? **c.** Est-ce qu'ils jouent au tennis ? **d.** Est-ce que tu aimes lire ? **e.** Habites-tu en Italie ? / Tu habites en Italie ?

❾ **a.** Quand **b.** Que **c.** Quelle **d.** Où **e.** Qui **f.** Comment (The extra word is **pourquoi**.)

❿ **1.** d **2.** f **3.** a **4.** b **5.** c **6.** e

⓫ **a.** Who is this boy? **b.** Why isn't he watching this movie? **c.** How are you getting ('going') to Sylvain's tomorrow? **d.** Which dress are you wearing ('putting-on') to go to the party? **e.** When are you leaving on vacation? **f.** What's for lunch? / What are we eating for lunch?

⓬ **a.** Qu'écoutes-tu ? / Qu'est-ce que tu écoutes ? **b.** Où va Clarèle ? / Où Clarèle va-t-elle ? **c.** Qui est-elle ? **d.** Quand regardez-vous le film ? **e.** Pourquoi es-tu triste ?

12. The past

❶ **a.** allons **b.** Allez **c.** vont **d.** vais **e.** Vas

❷ **a.** regarder **b.** avoir / donner **c.** avoir / finir **d.** être / descendre **e.** remplir **f.** avoir / répondre

❸ 1st group: chanter, ranger; 2nd group: définir, nourrir; 3rd group: apprendre, boire, vendre, répondre, savoir, entendre, pouvoir

❹ **a.** apprendre (3) **b.** lire (3) **c.** manger (1) **d.** venir (2) **e.** se lever (1) **f.** espérer (1) **g.** faire (3)

❺ **1.** détester, détesté **2.** perdre, perdu **3.** lire, lu **4.** finir, fini **5.** aimer, aimé **6.** réussir, réussi

❻ **a.** tu as attendu → you (have) waited **b.** nous avons regardé → we (have) looked/watched **c.** vous avez vendu → you (have) sold **d.** ils ont bâti → they (have) built **e.** j'ai répondu → I (have) answered **f.** elle a fait → she (has) done

❼ **a.** jeté **b.** envoyé **c.** restés **d.** lu **e.** tombée **f.** espéré

❽ **a.** suis **b.** avons **c.** sont **d.** as **e.** a **f.** sommes

❾ **a.** avons fini **b.** a voulu **c.** avez fait **d.** est allée **e.** Ils sont partis **f.** ai vendu

❿ **a.** compris **b.** bu **c.** lu **d.** fait **e.** pu **f.** écrit

13. Talking about time & weather

❶ **a.** Je ne vais pas à l'école en été. **b.** Loïc va au Portugal en automne. **c.** Noël est en hiver. **d.** Cora aime manger des glaces au printemps.

❷ **Il y a:** b–c–f–h **Il fait**: a–d–e–g

❸ **a.** Il y a du vent. **b.** Il fait beau. / Il y a du soleil. **c.** Il pleut. / Il y a de la pluie. / Il fait mauvais. / Il y a des nuages. **d.** Il fait chaud. **e.** Il fait froid.

❹ **a.** à **b.** De... à... **c.** pendant **d.** Entre **e.** jusqu'à

❺ **a.** I go to bed around 10 p.m. **b.** I will call you in 10 minutes. **c.** I am coming home before noon. **d.** I do my homework after dinner. **e.** I have been at the swimming pool since this morning.

❻ **a.** septembre **b.** février **c.** juillet **d.** juin **e.** décembre **f.** janvier

❼ **a.** Aujourd'hui, nous sommes le 2 février 2012.
b. Aujourd'hui, nous sommes le 5 septembre 2010.
c. Aujourd'hui, nous sommes le 29 avril 2005.
d. Aujourd'hui, nous sommes le 1er août 2003.
e. Aujourd'hui, nous sommes le 15 juin 2013.

❽ **a.** Je ne vais pas à l'école le samedi. **b.** Je vais au cinéma dimanche. **c.** J'ai géographie le mardi. **d.** Je vais chez mes grands-parents le mercredi. **e.** Elle va chez le dentiste vendredi.

❾ **a.** souvent **b.** souvent **c.** généralement **d.** toujours **e.** généralement

❿ **a.** Ils ne téléphonent jamais... **b.** Nous n'écoutons jamais... **c.** Vous ne finissez jamais... **d.** Tu n'entends jamais... **e.** Je ne perds jamais...

⓫ **a.** soir **b.** Aujourd'hui **c.** maintenant **d.** prochaine **e.** hier **f.** matin

14. Talking about location

❶ **a.** entre **b.** dans **c.** loin de **d.** sur **e.** sous **f.** devant

2 **a.** The toilet/bathroom is between the bedroom and the kitchen. **b.** Your coat is in the garage. **c.** The cinema is very far from our house! We have to go there by car. **d.** The pizza is on the kitchen table. **e.** The dog is hiding under my parents' bed. **f.** Claire is on the sofa, in front of the television.

3 **a.** devant **b.** derrière **c.** sous **d.** dans **e.** sur **f.** entre **g.** à gauche / à côté **h.** à droite / à côté

4 **a.** dans **b.** à côté de **c.** à gauche **d.** en dessous **e.** en face de **f.** au milieu de

5 **a.** à **b.** en **c.** au **d.** aux **e.** en **f.** à

6 **a.** Aiko habite à Nagoya au Japon. **b.** Elvis habite à Tupelo aux États-Unis. **c.** Myriam habite à Boismorand en France. **d.** Marco habite à Cascais au Portugal. **e.** Chloé habite à Bruges en Belgique. **f.** Louis habite à Québec au Canada.

7 **a.** Corinne is at home. **b.** Carlos is going to Paul's on Saturday. **c.** Oh no! My bag is at your grandmother's! **d.** The children are playing in the park. **e.** Éloïse is in the hospital!

8 **a.** à l' **b.** à la **c.** chez **d.** au **e.** chez **f.** à la

9 **a.** la pharmacie **b.** les urgences **c.** le dentiste **d.** l'église **e.** la bibliothèque **f.** l'hôpital

10 **Je vais:** a–b–e–h **Je viens:** c–d–f–g

15. Making commands & requests

1 **a.** Mange **b.** Ayez **c.** Finissons **d.** Obéissez **e.** Lave **f.** Vendons

2 **a.** Arrête **b.** Prenez **c.** Écoute **d.** Soyons **e.** Veuillez **f.** Pars

3 **a.** Mangez votre pain ! **b.** Sors de la salle de bain ! **c.** Allons à la bibliothèque ! **d.** Regardons un film ! **e.** Lisez l'exercice p.16. **f.** Prends un biscuit !

4 **a.** Ne téléphone pas à Sophie. **b.** Ne donnez pas votre adresse. **c.** Ne finissez pas les oranges. **d.** Ne perds pas tes clés. **e.** Ne choisissons pas une maison aujourd'hui.

5 **a.** Don't phone Sophie. **b.** Don't give your address. **c.** Don't finish the oranges. **d.** Don't lose your keys. **e.** Let's not choose a house today.

6 **a.** la **b.** la **c.** le **d.** les **e.** le

7 **a.** Appelez-les ! **b.** Donne-les ! **c.** Vendez-la ! **d.** Prends-la ! **e.** Remplissez-la ! **f.** Finis-le !

8 **a.** Douchez-vous ! **b.** Levons-nous ! **c.** Couche-toi ! **d.** Promène-toi ! **e.** Réveillez-vous !

9 droite *right* – gauche *left* – devant *in front of* – derrière *behind* – tourner *to turn* – traverser *to cross* – continuer *to carry on*

10 **a.** Tournez à droite après l'église. **b.** Continue tout droit. **c.** La pharmacie est derrière le musée. **d.** La gare est en face de la piscine. **e.** Prenez la première rue à gauche.

16. The future

1 **a.** prendrons **b.** partiront **c.** achèterai **d.** demandera **e.** appelleras **f.** lirez

2 **a.** regardera **b.** rendront **c.** bâtirez **d.** descendrons **e.** danseras **f.** choisirai

3 arrivera – passera – iront – mangeront – partira – verra – viendras – demandera – irai – répondra

4 **a.** saura **b.** Viendras **c.** serons **d.** devras **e.** Ferez **f.** verront

5 **a.** viendrons **b.** verrai **c.** pourrez **d.** fera **e.** devront **f.** courras

6 je vais – tu vas – il/elle va – nous allons – vous allez – ils/elles vont

7 **a.** allez rater **b.** allons voir **c.** va écouter **d.** vont manger **e.** vais téléphoner **f.** vont choisir

8 **a.** Je n'irai pas... **b.** Nous n'allons pas voir... **c.** Ils ne vont pas manger... **d.** Vous n'allez pas visiter... **e.** Audrey ne va pas prendre...

9 **a.** Je ne regarderai pas la télé. **b.** Ils vont attendre le bus. **c.** Sonia ne va pas perdre son sac à main. **d.** Le train ne partira pas à 10 heures. **e.** Philippe va répondre aux questions.

10

	1	2	3	4	5	6	7	8	9	10	11	12	13
a	L	I	R	A	S				F	E	R	A	
b	È				A				I				C
c	V		V	O	U	D	R	O	N	T			R
d	E		I		R		E		I		E		O
e	R		E		A	I	M	E	R	A	S		I
f	A		N		I		P		O		P		R
g	S		D				L		N		É		A
h			R				I		S	E	R	A	I
i		P	E	I	N	D	R	A			E		
j			Z				A	I	M	E	R	A	I
k											E		
l		D	E	M	A	N	D	E	R	E	Z		

17. Adverbs

1 **a.** joliment **b.** tristement **c.** grand → grande → grandement **d.** léger → légère → légèrement **e.** joyeux → joyeuse → joyeusement **f.** gentiment **g.** suffisamment

2 **a.** meilleur (ADJ) **b.** gentiment (ADV) **c.** bon (ADJ) **d.** rapidement (ADV) **e.** bien (ADV) **f.** mauvais (ADJ) **g.** jolie (ADJ)

3 **a.** généralement **b.** toujours **c.** parfois **d.** rarement **e.** toujours

4 **a.** Je vais souvent au cinéma. **b.** Ma sœur mange tout le temps du chocolat. **c.** Ils/Elles ne lisent jamais. **d.** Henry se lève parfois à 7 heures. **e.** Le professeur ne dit jamais bonjour.

5 **a.** jamais **b.** demain **c.** tôt **d.** souvent **e.** tard **f.** Hier **g.** bientôt

6 **a.** I never go to the museum: it's too boring! **b.** Rachel will go to her grandparents' tomorrow. **c.** You have to get up early: the train leaves at 6 a.m.! **d.** We often go to the cinema because we love seeing new movies. **e.** You can't come home after midnight: that's too late! **f.** Yesterday we went to the dentist: it was horrible! **g.** Hurry up! The bus is going to leave soon!

7 **a.** partout – nulle part **b.** là-bas **c.** en bas **d.** en haut **e.** loin **f.** dehors

8 **a.** assez **b.** plus de **c.** trop **d.** un peu **e.** beaucoup

9 **a.** Quand **b.** Pourquoi **c.** Qui **d.** Comment **e.** Où **f.** Combien

10 **a.** Il a bu son café rapidement. **b.** Je ne vais pas souvent au cinéma. **c.** Sylvain est vraiment très gentil. **d.** Sa grand-mère va beaucoup mieux. **e.** Léa ne mange jamais de pain. **f.** Ils sont allés au cinéma avant-hier. / Avant-hier, ils sont allés au cinéma.

18. Making comparisons

1 **1.** e **2.** g **3.** a **4.** f **5.** d **6.** c **7.** b

2 **a.** mignonne → cute **b.** géniale → great **c.** intéressante → interesting **d.** affreuse → awful **e.** inutile → useless **f.** intelligente → intelligent

3 **a.** Les mathématiques sont plus utiles que le sport. **b.** L'histoire est moins intéressante que la chimie. **c.** Le sport est plus amusant que le français. **d.** La géographie est aussi ennuyeuse que la musique. **e.** L'informatique est moins fatigante que le sport.

4 **a.** The table is taller than the chair. **b.** Louis is less kind than / not as kind as Julian. **c.** Julie's cake is as bad as yours! **d.** This dress is prettier than that one. **e.** The blue bag is as light as the red one.

5 **Adjectives:** gentil, mauvais, jeune, heureuse
Adverbs: mieux, lentement, gentiment, doucement

6 **a.** rarement **b.** prudemment **c.** calmement **d.** rapidement **e.** énormément **f.** gentiment

7 **a.** la **b.** le **c.** les **d.** le **e.** la

8 **a.** intéressant **b.** lourds **c.** propres **d.** gentilles **e.** vieille

9 **a.** le meilleur **b.** plus timides que **c.** la plus généreuse **d.** le pire (film) **e.** plus jeune que

10 **a.** Ce livre est le pire livre de la bibliothèque. **b.** Davy est plus petit que Geoffrey. **c.** Edwige est la fille la plus heureuse de l'école. **d.** Ninon est moins triste qu'Olivier. **e.** Ces garçons sont les meilleurs joueurs de l'équipe.

19. Linking words

1 **a.** mais **b.** Ni… ni **c.** Toutefois **d.** d'ailleurs **e.** donc **f.** ou

2 **a.** donc / c'est pourquoi **b.** car **c.** Soit… soit… **d.** et **e.** c'est pourquoi / donc

3 **1.** d **2.** a **3.** f **4.** g **5.** e **6.** c **7.** b

4 **a.** dès que → as soon as **b.** parce que → because **c.** Quand → when **d.** puisque → since, because **e.** Si → if **f.** Depuis que → since

5 **1.** d **2.** f **3.** a **4.** g **5.** b **6.** e **7.** c

6 **a.** Premièrement **b.** Deuxièmement **c.** Ensuite **d.** Finalement **e.** De plus **f.** Par contre **g.** En résumé

7 **a.** car / parce que **b.** Toutefois / Pourtant / Cependant / Or **c.** Dès que / Quand **d.** Si **e.** mais / toutefois / pourtant **f.** par exemple

20. Review

1 **a.** dix **b.** cinquante-quatre **c.** cent **d.** deux cent cinq **e.** six **f.** vingt-cinq **g.** cinq cent quatre-vingt-neuf **h.** neuf cent quatre-vingt-dix-neuf

2 **a.** Mon père est dans le grenier. **b.** Ses frères sont dans la cuisine. **c.** Ses parents sont avocats. **d.** Sa grand-mère est dentiste. **e.** Ta sœur est dans la salle de bain. **f.** Votre mère est professeur.

3 **a.** les bonbons **b.** le gâteau **c.** la tomate **d.** le pain **e.** l'eau / le verre d'eau **f.** la banane **g.** le poisson / le dîner **h.** le lit **i.** la table **j.** la chaise **k.** le canapé **l.** la lampe

4

A	C	E	G	J	Q	A	E	V	E
D	F	M	H	L	P	E	T	I	T
E	J	O	L	I	M	A	D	E	R
D	R	C	C	M	L	J	U	U	F
I	D	H	E	U	R	E	U	X	D
F	D	E	B	B	Z	U	Z	W	C
F	V	A	F	B	U	N	D	V	X
I	D	G	H	V	T	E	B	E	G
C	N	E	E	H	I	F	E	R	T
I	L	I	U	G	L	É	G	E	R
L	O	U	R	D	E	J	A	W	I
E	O	A	E	R	S	G	E	T	S
B	M	A	U	V	A	I	S	H	T
S	A	C	X	D	U	P	E	F	E

5 **a.** allemand (m.) (allemande, f.) → l'Allemagne **b.** chinois (m.) (chinoise, f.) → la Chine **c.** suisse (m./f.) → la Suisse **d.** espagnol (m.) (espagnole, f.) → l'Espagne **e.** japonais (m.) (japonaise, f.) → le Japon **f.** néerlandais (m.) (néerlandaise, f.) → les Pays-Bas / la Hollande

6 **1.** d (un chat) **2.** a (un serpent) **3.** b (des chevaux) **4.** e (une lapine) **5.** g (une tortue) **6.** c (une souris) **7.** f (une chienne)

7 **a.** Il est deux heures et quart. / Il est deux heures quinze.
b. Il est quinze heures vingt-cinq. / Il est trois heures vingt-cinq de l'après-midi.
c. Il est neuf heures moins le quart. / Il est vingt heures quarante-cinq. / Il est huit heures quarante-cinq du soir.
d. Il est huit heures trente. / Il est huit heures et demie.
e. Il est quatre/seize heures dix.
f. Il est cinq heures cinquante-cinq. / Il est six heures moins cinq.

8 Present tense conjugations:

écouter	finir
j'écoute	je finis
tu écoutes	tu finis
il/elle écoute	il/elle finit
nous écoutons	nous finissons
vous écoutez	vous finissez
ils/elles écoutent	ils/elles finissent
vendre	**être**
je vends	je suis
tu vends	tu es
il/elle vend	il/elle est
nous vendons	nous sommes
vous vendez	vous êtes
ils/elles vendent	ils/elles sont
avoir	**aller**
j'ai	je vais
tu as	tu vas
il/elle a	il/elle va
nous avons	nous allons
vous avez	vous allez
ils/elles ont	ils/elles vont
appeler	**prendre**
j'appelle	je prends
tu appelles	tu prends
il/elle appelle	il/elle prend
nous appelons	nous prenons
vous appelez	vous prenez
ils/elles appellent	ils/elles prennent
faire	
je fais	
tu fais	
il/elle fait	
nous faisons	
vous faites	
ils/elles font	

9 **a.** Comment t'appelles-tu ? / Comment vous appelez-vous ? **b.** Où habites-tu ? / Où habitez-vous ? **c.** Qui va au musée avec toi ? / Qui va au musée avec vous ? **d.** Quand vient Sophie ? **e.** Combien de chemises as-tu ? / Combien de chemises avez-vous ? **f.** Pourquoi es-tu fatiguée ? / Pourquoi êtes-vous fatiguée ?

10 **a.** Léo a cinq pantalons noirs. **b.** Bérénice a dix chapeaux roses. **c.** Maël a vingt casquettes vertes. **d.** Sasha n'a pas de robe rouge. / Sasha n'a aucune robe rouge. **e.** Colin et Marie ont trois chemises marron. **f.** Tu as / Vous avez sept pyjamas violets.

11 **a.** Caroline est allée au cinéma hier. **b.** Francis a mangé les fraises. **c.** J'ai lu tous les livres. **d.** Ils/Elles ont adoré ce musée. **e.** Tu as fait tes devoirs. / Vous avez fait vos devoirs. **f.** Ils/Elles ont vendu leur maison.

12 **a.** Chantal et Clément adorent la natation. / Chantal et Clément adorent nager. **b.** Tu n'aimes pas le tennis. / Tu n'aimes pas jouer au tennis. **c.** J'aime la marche. / J'aime marcher. **d.** Nous détestons la gymnastique. / Nous détestons faire de la gymnastique. **e.** Manon aime le rugby. / Manon aime jouer au rugby.

13 **a.** Noël **b.** Pâques **c.** une fête **d.** français **e.** zéro **f.** août **g.** ta mère **h.** une secrétaire **i.** une leçon **j.** bientôt **k.** un vélo **l.** un hôtel **m.** vous êtes **n.** américain **o.** les pâtes

14 **a.** F **b.** F **c.** F **d.** M / P **e.** F **f.** M / P **g.** M **h.** F **i.** M **j.** F / P

15 **le:** salon, garage; **l':** hôtel, entrée; **la:** salle à manger, cuisine; **les:** toilettes, chambres

16 **a.** jolie **b.** heureuse **c.** légère **d.** grande **e.** canadienne **f.** vieille **g.** bonne **h.** amoureuse

17 **a.** Mon **b.** ses **c.** mon **d.** ma **e.** ta **f.** leurs

18 **a.** Nous **b.** J' **c.** J'/Elle/Il **d.** tu **e.** Vous **f.** Ils/Elles

19 **a.** m' **b.** nous **c.** lui **d.** vous **e.** lui **f.** t' **g.** leur

20 **a.** quatrième **b.** vingtième **c.** quatorzième **d.** trente-deuxième **e.** centième **f.** soixantième **g.** douzième

21 **a.** nous laverons **b.** s'habillera **c.** se lèveront **d.** te brosseras **e.** vous réveillerez **f.** me promènerai

Félicitations ! You've reached the end of this workbook! Now it's time to assess how you did by counting up the icons of each type for all the lessons. Make sure that you've put the sub-totals from each lesson in the boxes below, then add them up to find the total number for each of the three icons.

1. Alphabet & pronunciation
2. More on pronunciation
3. Nouns & articles
4. Pronouns & more on articles
5. Adjectives
6. Possession & likes and dislikes
7. The present tense
8. Numbers & time
9. More on the present tense
10. More on pronouns
11. Types of sentences
12. The past
13. Talking about time & weather
14. Talking about location
15. Making commands & requests
16. The future
17. Adverbs
18. Making comparisons
19. Linking words
20. Review

Total (all lessons)

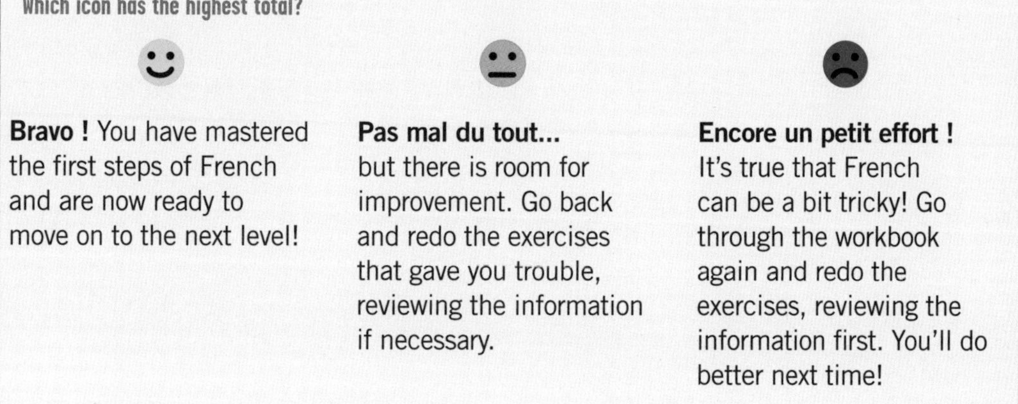

Which icon has the highest total?

Bravo ! You have mastered the first steps of French and are now ready to move on to the next level!

Pas mal du tout... but there is room for improvement. Go back and redo the exercises that gave you trouble, reviewing the information if necessary.

Encore un petit effort ! It's true that French can be a bit tricky! Go through the workbook again and redo the exercises, reviewing the information first. You'll do better next time!

Illustration credits:

Shutterstock: Aleutie: 6h; Alex Gorka: 40 (chiffres); Alexander Ryabintsev: 29 (drapeaux bord de page); Anastasiia Kucherenko: 66b; ankomando: 6b, 48; Annasunny24: 72h, 104h; Becris: 107; benchart: 111 (lit); bilha golan: 114 (cinéma); bioraven: 22 (pain), 111 (pain); Blablo101: 26hg, 26hm, 26hd, 26bg, 26bd, 90b; Bplanet: 8b; Chernoskutov Mikhail: 78h (point d'interrogation); Colorlife: 56, 102h; createvil: 67g; Delices: 63 (pomme); Diana Hlevnjak: 85h; Dooder: 50h; elenabsl: 101; Elvetica: 19b; Evellean: 18 (figure 6), 95 (chien), 110b (avocats); Faber14: 84b; feelplus: 76, 112h; Filip Bjorkman: 10; Fotinia: 35 (pyjama), 51m; GoodVector: 34; graphic-line: 15; Gurza: 21hd, 59b; happymay: 35 (chaussettes); HelenStock: 45; HieroGraphic: 21hg; honglouwawa: 39; Iconic Bestiary: 31h, 94; Igogosha: 13; in_dies_magis: 57; Incomible: 47, 68h, 81b; Iurii_A: 118b; Ivan_Nikulin: 64; jabkitticha: 31b; jesadaphorn: 46 (figure 3), 67d (ampoule), 67d (homme); Julia Tim: 38h, 117b, 118h; karawan: 75b (cartons); KissBeetle: 49 (main), 50b; Kriukova Olya: 78m (vignettes x3); KY726871: 42; LanaN: 74 (chaise et lampe), 111 (lampe); lanitta: 35 (valise); LineTale: 77; liskus: 38b; Liudmila Dobraya: 21bg, 58b, 111 (tomate); Lorelyn Medina: 111 (canapé); Lucky Team Studio: 9h; lyeyee: 70b; Macrovector: 22 (glace), 32, 37h, 46 (figure 1), 49hd, 46 (figure 4), 60h, 72b, 99h, 105, 106, 108, 115; MakaCz: 63 (jus d'orange); MANGA MEDIA: 103; Manon_Labe: 96; MarinaMay: 117h; Marish: 83b; mart: 22 (jambon); Meilun: 11b, 86, 119; Merfin: 18 (figure 2); mghstars: 51d; mhatzapa: 12; milo827: 24b; miniwide: 59h; Minur: 111 (bonbons); mirrra3: 89 ; Miuky: 116b; miumi: 100; Mix3r: 68b, 70h, 71; MyClipArtStore.com: 104b; mything: 111 (banane); Nadya_Art: 91hg, 112b; NGvozdeva: 79; NokHoOkNoi: 111 (table); Nong Amory: 21bd; NotionPic: 22 (poisson), 65, 90, 111 (poisson); Oceans: 41, 52, 53; Older Brother: 111 (verre d'eau); Olga1818: 3h, 8h, 22h, 24h, 60b, 62, 82h, 87b, 102b, 109 (jeune fille), 114 (personnages), 116h; olillia: 99b; Oxy_gen: 55; Padma Sanjaya: 18 (figure 5); palasha: 61h; PODIS: 58h; Polyudova Yulia: 16; Pretty Vectors: 98; primiaou: 61b; Rimma Rii: 95 (plantes); Rimma Z: 93; Rosa Puchalt: 87h, 111 (gateau); Sentavio: 30 (chat), 30 (chien); Sibiryanka: 51g; SLdesign: 9b; SlyBrowney: 68m; Smart Design: 88; SofiaV: 80b; Spreadthesign: 30 (souris), 109 (arbres); Stocklifemax: 46 (figure 6); Studio Barcelona: 22 (pomme); Syquallo: 11h; takiwa: 46 (figure 5 – boîte aux lettres); Tarikdiz: 18 (figure 1); tn-prints: 5b; Tomacco: 33; tynyuk: 19h; vasabii: 66h; Vector pro: 28; venimo: 75h, 78h (sac), 81h, 85b; Vetreno: 83h; VikiVector: 73; Virinaflora: 78b; Visual Generation: 37b; Volha Shaukavets: 54; WWWoronin: 3b; Yurchenko Yulia: 14; Zubada: 63b; zzveillust: 74 (poisson), 111 (chaise). **DR:** 4, 17h, 17b, 18 (figure 3), 18 (figure 4), 22 (bouteille), 28 (drapeaux tableau), 35 (jupe), 35 (casquette), 35 (chemise), 43h, 43b, 44 (horloges et réveils), 46 (figure 2), 46 (figure 5 – enveloppe), 69, 80h, 82b, 84h (flèches), 90hd, 92, 97, 110h, 110b (balance).

Legal deposit: March 2018

Publication number: 4320 - December 2023

ISBN: 978-2-7005-0987-8

www.assimil.com

Printed in Roumanie by Master Print

Designed by: MediaSarbacane

Layout: Grégoire Chauvière for Lunedit